WE COULD'VE HAD A GREAT DATE IF IT WEREN'T FOR YOU

A GUIDE TO AUTHENTIC DATING

BY

BRUCE DERMAN, PH.D.

This book is a work of non-fiction. Names and places have been changed to protect the privacy of all individuals. The events and situations are true.

ISBN: 1-4107-9336-2 (e-book)
ISBN: 1-4107-9335-4 (Paperback)

This book is printed on acid free paper.

1stBooks – rev. 02/23/04

DEDICATION

To my love buddy, Marla who showed me what love really is and what it means to be with a real woman

ACKNOWLEDGEMENTS

I want to thank every woman I have ever dated for the experiences they provided me in developing my perspective and attitude on dating. They were all part of my dating journey.

I want to thank my many editors, including Sylvia Cary, who played a part in forming this book, and to Lois Winsen, who truly believed in it, and Marla Gorlick who brought final closure to it at last.

I also want to thank Jed Bauman for all his formatting assistance.

TABLE OF CONTENTS

PART I

INTRODUCTION

CHAPTER 1

ENDING THE DATING ORDEAL

Ordeal (definition): A severe trial or experience.
-Merriam-Webster's Collegiate Dictionary

When did dating get to be such an ordeal? Two people come together, pretend, pose, hide, sit behind a stream of judgments about what's right or wrong, good or bad, acceptable or unacceptable about the other. After years of this, no wonder most of the country's 77 million adult single agree that:

- Dating is uncomfortable
- Dating is painful
- Dating is futile
- Dating is a waste of time
- Dating is boring
- Dating is difficult
- Dating is something you just have to put up with
- Dating is an ordeal

Everybody's Got a Dating War Story

When a Los Angeles radio station asked listeners to call in with their worst dating experiences, the phone lines lit up. It seemed everybody had a dating nightmare they wanted to share with the world. Perhaps you have one, too.

One 35-year-old man from Los Angeles called in to say he had made Internet contact with a girl who lived in Dallas. After two months of conversation he agreed to fly out there to see her. He expected her to meet him at the Dallas airport, but when he got there, she wasn't at the arrival gate. After roaming around the airport for two hours and calling her place, he flew back home. Soon after, she e-mailed him saying in her defense that she had been at the airport, and it was his mistake that he didn't see her.

The talk radio interviewer remarked, "Boy, that was one expensive date!" The man said, "In many ways. It blew me out of dating for several months."

Dating can be painful stuff – for men and women alike.

Her Story

"My friend called to tell me about an ad she saw in the paper for a singles dance. She wanted me to go with her. I said, I'm not sure I can handle another meat-market dance. I'm sick of mingling in crowded, smoke-filled rooms making small talk with guys while the band blares, and I can barely hear what they're saying. Not that it really matters, since the conversation is usually meaningless platitudes. Sometimes I'll go to a singles dance alone. I circulate so I don't miss out on any possibilities. On a good night, three men take my number. Maybe one won't throw it in the trash. The last time I went, I gave the men a quick once-over and headed for the door. One fellow said to me, Where are you going? The night is young. Not slowing my pace, I blurted out, But I'm not getting any younger. Outside, I had a good laugh and went home. Unfortunately, the laughter didn't last long. I was soon back at another singles dance, uttering my usual complaint, "Dating sucks!"

His Story

"Another date. I'm not sure if I can get up the energy to dress, let alone get in the car and drive twenty miles. How many dates have I had this year? 15? 20? 30? I've lost count. After a while they all seem to blend together. God, it seems like I've told the same stories so many times it makes me want to throw up just listening to myself. I was married…I went to school…I'm interested in…How many versions can I tell? After all, I only have one life. The only thing more boring than my own repetitive lament is listening to my date's stories. It gets so I know what the woman is going to say before she even opens her mouth. Will I ever see the light at the end of this dating tunnel?"

In *The Unofficial Guide to Dating Again,* author Tina Tessina, Ph.D., takes the view that maybe we should stop calling it dating, since the D-word has come to have such a negative connotation. She recommended calling it squirrel hunting as a less offensive label. One woman shared with me that many of the single people she meets prefer using the term "hanging out" in order to avoid the more definitive statement "we are dating."

Shmuley Boteach, a rabbi who works with singles, takes it one step further in his book, *Why Can't I Fall in Love?* "Single men and women of our time," he writes, "seem increasingly to be made of Teflon. Men and women can't seem to stick together. We go out on dates conscientiously, relentlessly, almost obsessively. We have become Olympic gold medalists of the event called dating, and yet many of us are curiously unaffected by the experience."

I agree that a definite degree of numbing occurs, but even numbing indicates that people are being affected. In fact, I have found most everyone who enters the world of dating is struggling with a series of dilemmas. The first is, "If I don't date, I won't meet anyone, so I have to get out there." The second is, "If I do date, I'll meet unsuitable people." The third is, "Whoever I meet will be examining me under a microscope, and what if I don't pass?" In order to resolve these dilemmas and not view dating negatively, we must understand how we create all this angst in the first place.

Factors Leading to the Dating Ordeal

There are eight factors single people are either unaware of, ignore, or oppose that lead to the dating ordeal. These result in regarding dating as a necessary evil to endure as we wend our way to the Promised Land. While the promises we are seeking might vary, the discomfort with the dating game does not. The factors are:

1. Opposing the integrity of dating
2. Hiding the substance of dating
3. Insisting on being surprised
4. Only valuing a relationship with The One
5. Being seduced by the dating myths
6. Framing relationships as good or bad, and successful or unsuccessful
7. Not respecting and being accountable for the relationship space you are currently in
8. The belief that the lover you desire is lost

1. Integrity of Dating

Dating is a series of tests and judgments followed by acceptance or rejection. Though you hope for acceptance, for the most part you will more than likely experience rejection.

It is said that a man has to risk the possibility of rejection 150 times before he gets a woman to go to bed with him. On the female side, ask any woman how many times some man has told her he was going to call, and didn't.

As it stands now, when you go out on a first date, I estimate the chances are 60% that one of you will reject the other by the end of the evening. I base that percentage figure on my personal observations, thirty-five years of professional experience, and on many discussions with other therapists and friends. From this I have come to view dating as a judgmental gauntlet. This is not a negative assessment, as you might think, but one based on reality. Rejection goes with the territory, and the more you dread this truth and run from it, the more dating will continue to be an ordeal.

Here's a typical dating scenario filled with testing and judgments. On a second date, following dinner, the bill arrives. The man who initiated the meeting realizes it's too soon to ask for any help from his date, and besides, she wouldn't regard him as "cool" if he did. So he pulls out his trusty credit card. His date then asks, "Can I help you pay?"

Liking the sound of those words, but certainly not trusting them, he responds, "Whatever makes you comfortable. "Her face turns cold as the trap is set. He asks, "What's wrong?" She says, "I was expecting you to pay because you invited me. I always ask just to be polite, but you are the first man to take me up on it."

Mr. Dater walks away puzzled, thinking to himself, "She insisted she wasn't into game playing. She told me she wasn't a princess. She said she considers herself honest and not materialistic. What the heck's going on?" A voice in his head responds, "Sorry, pal, you flunked the date."

The voice of rejection can be expressed in many forms, and anywhere along the dating relationship path. Some rejections are direct. Others are garbled, vague, disguised, or cryptic. At times the rejection is delivered in person, but it may also come via phone, e-mail, or through spokespersons.

Imagine the horror and chagrin of one woman when, after 12 years of marriage, she received an e-mail saying, "You have been great for 12 years, and I now need to move on in order to be happy." Another woman, after three months of intimate times and family get-togethers, expressions of love, and involved discussions of plans for the future, received a phone call that ended with the other person saying, "I just can't do this anymore my feelings are flat."

See if you can relate to any of these rejection scenarios.

You think you're having a great date with an attractive man. He says he'll call, but you never hear from him again.

You really like the personality and looks of the date you met for dinner, and you are open about your interest. But she says it won't work because she is only attracted to WASPs, and since you are Hispanic, Jewish, Black or whatever, you just don't make the cut.

You find her very attractive and say so. Your date replies that she doesn't have the same feeling for you. You say, "What does that mean?" She responds, "I don't know. It's just a feeling."

You express an interest in him/her. Your date replies that you are not The One. When you ask how that conclusion arose from just a few exchanges, your date replies, "It's not you. You're great, really. The problem is with me."

2. Dating in the Dark—Hiding Out on the Date

A big part of what makes dating difficult is that so much of it goes on in the dark.

You may think the lights are on and the acoustics are fine where you are drinking coffee or eating dinner, but they are certainly not shining on who you are really with, nor will you be able to hear the stream of judgment calls going on in your date's mind. You will be able to hear the noise of your own judgments, but you may find yourself spending most of your time struggling with what to do with these thoughts.

While most people consider the giving or receiving of judgments to be a major problem, and believe the solution is to be totally non-judgmental, I disagree. For one thing, such an event will never happen. Judgments are, and always will be, an integral part of dating. The key is to accept that and stop hiding our judgments.

From the moment we make contact with a potential date, hear each other's voice, the tone and pacing of it, judging begins. By the time you make it to the first date, it really ramps up.

He: Hi. (*Her looks are only so-so.*)

She: Hi. (*He's not a cool dresser.*)

He: What do you do? Secretary? (*Probably not too smart.*)

She: Have you ever been married? Twice? (*Loser!*)

Dating, like Shakespeare's *The Taming of the Shrew*, is a play within a play. In the foreground are the presentable and acceptable activities of dating: having dinner, sharing general information, maintaining a comfortable dialogue, going to the movies, or dancing. Typically, all of the judgments going on in each dater's head during these activities are never shared up front and remain in the background. Hidden from view are endless internal discussions, judgments, and decisions concerning the possibilities of this date.

"I'm not sure I'm attracted enough."

"Where is his sense of humor?"

"I'm getting bored already and it has only been 30 minutes."

"I guess he isn't too bad."

"I'm missing that special feeling."

"I think I like her more than she likes me."

"I wish we could move this along faster."

For those of you who remember the Woody Allen movie *Annie Hall*, this contrast of what is verbally presented and what is hidden is wonderfully played out in a conversation between the two characters, Annie and Alvy. Fascinating monologues went on in their heads, while their nonsense conversation occupied our attention.

Annie: I sort of dabble around with photographs. (*I sound like a jerk.*)

Alvy: Your pictures are wonderful. *(You are a great looking girl.)*

Annie: I'd like to take a serious course in it. *(He probably thinks I'm a yo-yo)*

lvy: Photography is a new art form. *(I wonder what she looks like naked.)*

lvy: The medium enters in as a condition of the art form itself. *(I don't know what I am saying. She senses I'm shallow.)*

Annie: Well, to me it is all instinctive. *(God! I hope he doesn't turn out to be a schmuck like the others.)*

Alvy: Still, you need a set of aesthetic guidelines to put it in a social perspective. *(Christ, I sound like FM radio. Relax.)*

This split between our internal voice and our external expression is designed to hide our judgments about ourselves and about our dates. As long as you feel this need to split yourself, you will rarely be able to enjoy your dates. In fact, as long as you are having intense dialogues in your head, and pretending you are not, most of you will hardly be able to show up on the date. Then, on top of that, you will probably be worried as in the *Annie Hall* scene about the judgments your date is making about you. As a result you will be lucky to have 30% of you available to be truly with the other. The only way to get around this is to learn to express your hidden judgments. The more you are able to share, the less pressure you will feel to hide and pretend.

Even at the end of dates, judgments are still relatively sealed and leak out only in disguised rhetoric, such as, "See you sometime," "I'm pretty busy right now," or "Not sure we are a match." It is left to the receiving person to figure out what all that means.

Daters typically find themselves drowning in these kinds of nebulous responses. It doesn't change much even if you ask for more clarity. It is truly dating in the dark when you are left to wonder if it was your looks, your personality, or your career that failed to pass inspection. Sometimes you will feel you have been stabbed with a velvet knife.

Other times you may feel you've been hit over the head with a sledgehammer.

Such vague replies are maddening, but are you prepared for total clarity? David had gone out several times with a charming woman before he asked her if she was ready to become more intimate. She said no, explaining, "You're too old, too short, and too bald."

Such a remark might well be considered offensive. But David was able to tell her truthfully that he appreciated her candor, after which the two said goodnight and went their separate ways. "It was an interesting experience," he later confided to a friend.

"There was something refreshing about hearing the truth for once, instead of getting the usual excuse – "I'm kind of busy right now.""

For many this would be more than you'd want to know, so dating in the dark is the only option.

Another aspect that promotes dating in the dark is that your date usually sends only their representative—the part of themselves they believe is most likely to appeal to you.

Chances are you're doing the same thing.

Comedian Chris Rock addressed this with the comment, "Everyone who dates lies, because none of us believe that anyone would want who we really are and what we look like. So you gotta lie. In fact, women lie the most. What woman would go out on a date with her real face and no makeup?" As a result, you are not meeting the real person, only their representative.

The need to send a representative adds to the dating ordeal due to the pressure to present yourself as someone you think your date will like. "You like smooth? I'll show you that. You like money? I'll dazzle you with that. You like sexy? I can do that, too."

There's pressure to keep up this pretense until the other one is hooked. Then the real scripts are pulled out, the ones that more truly reflect who we are. You start to see a controlling edge you never noticed before, or possibly a distant side. Even worse, you recognize a drinking problem or a gambling addiction. At this point you wonder what happened to the person you first met. The truth is, that person was never there. It was an illusion. When the illusion disappears, you may be left with a sense of despair. And to the degree you feel hurt by the exposure of who your date really is, you are again facing the dating ordeal.

3. The Surprise Factor

Dating is a hard enough journey when you can see. Traveling this road blind leads to a lot of falling and bumping along the way. Yet that is exactly what occurs when we constantly act surprised. "I didn't know dating a married man would be so difficult."

"He said he wasn't interested in a serious relationship, but I didn't think that had to do with me."

"She said that she was guarded, but I thought she would grow out of it."

Every time you act surprised you will find yourself on an emotional roller coaster screaming the woes of the dating ordeal.

4. Only Valuing a Relationship with "The One"

Almost every book focused on singles has one theme in common – how to obtain a relationship with The One. You may think this is not the goal for a lot of men, especially those seeking sexual conquests. There is some truth to that, but very few books are written with men in mind. Ultimately, men are also chasing The One who will change their lives forever. As Warren Farrell says in his book *Why Men Are The Way They Are*, "A man's primary fantasy is to be desired by all women," which leaves him longing for a woman other than the one he is currently seeing.

When finding The One is set out as a primary focus, certain assumptions fall into place: that all daters are looking for long-term committed relationships (LTCRs), that all daters should be looking for LTCRs, and that if these daters settle for less, it's because they are neurotic and riddled with low self-esteem. Shmuley Boteach, the author of *Why Can't I Fall in Love?* suggests that people who are not into this kind of relationship have become numb to their loneliness, and are desensitized by a wide range of cultural influences that say it is okay to live without love. The message is clear: find The One.

When daters want to jump ahead into committed relationships, many premature and often painful decisions are made. But despite my view that seeking only committed relationships limits a person's opportunities, it is inherent to the dating scene, setting up tremendous pressure and a counter-productive mind set. "Is he The One?" "Sorry, you are not The One." "I wish I could find The One." "Where do you find The One?" "I think all the good Ones are taken."

The pressure doesn't stop when you think you have found The One. Then the monologue changes to "What if he/she's really not The One?" "What if I made a mistake?" "Could I have been deceived?" By the time you exhaust all these questions about whether you have actually found The One, you will be well into the dating ordeal.

5. Being Seduced by the Dating Myths

One important thing pointed out in *The Unofficial Guide to Dating Again* by Tina Tessina is that the dating world is full of myths that have daters running around scared.

One is the scarcity myth, that all the good people are taken or don't even exist. Those who believe in this myth will feel fearful that with each passing day their opportunities for a meaningful relationship is quickly fading.

Another myth states that there is one great love waiting out there for you, and you need to find him/her. Believers of this disregard the fact that people grow and change, and somebody's one great love at twenty isn't what it would be at forty. Some mental health professionals think the ideal arrangement would be to go through four marriages in a lifetime in order to keep up with one's changing needs. The first marriage would be to learn to be with another person; the second would be to raise children; the third would be to live out one's unfulfilled dreams; and the last would be to have someone to share the final passage. While some people may be able to move through these phases with the same partner, others will require a change of partners.

The third myth is that all singles remaining in the dating pool are losers. The whole idea of "Loser" results from describing the dates that you don't know how to deal with, don't understand, or the dates you are no longer interested in because you've moved on. Believing in this myth will allow you to elevate your ego, but in the end will leave you frustrated and empty.

Still another popular myth relates to gender difference, positing that men are inferior to women on the relationship field of the dating world. In *What Really Works with Men*, Justin Sterling writes, "...women need to face facts that men don't know anything about managing intimate relationships." This leaves men seeing themselves as not enough and women feeling that the entire burden of a relationship rests on them. I believe men are underrated and women are overrated in the relationship area. The real distinction is whether we are talking to a person who can be honest about themselves or not. With honest, single people, I find hardly any real differences. Failure to recognize this view leads to a lot of inflated and deflated egos among the sexes.

Whether you subscribe to these myths or any others, you will find yourself under the influence of these beliefs, and they will run your dating life. As they lead you in endless circles, your dating ordeal will increase.

6. Framing All Relationships as Good or Bad, and Successful or Unsuccessful

We have been conditioned from birth that certain experiences represent success, while others are failures. Nowhere is this more apparent than in the dating world. We are always comparing our current dating pattern to some so-called acceptable standard.

The standard dictates that three dates is not a steady relationship. A two-year relationship is not marriage. Whatever you choose to compare with will lead you to seeing yourself as a failure.

For a date to be regarded as "successful," the consensus conditioning states that it must accomplish something or it's considered a failure.

Dating is supposed to lead to sex.

Dating is supposed to lead to a long-term relationship.

All dates have to go a certain way.

Dating has to be with the right person.

In the ceaseless process of ranking everyone and everything, we become fixed upon categorizing everything as *better than* or *worse than*. Our minds love to break experiences down into conditioned, judgmental opposites: good or bad, right or wrong, successful or unsuccessful. This mental exercise ends up barraging us with a constant stream of comparisons in regard to the dating experience. Now, the time spent together was either good or bad. The date behaved poorly or well. The relationship was a success or a failure.

Also, don't be fooled into thinking this lack of acceptance is only in regard to others. You will most likely do the same good-bad or right-wrong dance number on your own head. Every time you vote on someone's physical appearance as bad, you will probably be all over yourself whenever your own looks step outside that narrow line.

The same will be true in regard to intelligence. One day you will call a date stupid, and the next day you will come down on yourself for being really dumb. The more you succumb to rating everything as good or bad, the more you will find yourself trying to escape the bad.

You will live in fear that bad will triumph if you are not constantly vigilant. This will increase your dating ordeal ten-fold.

7. Not Respecting the Relationship You Are Ready For (If Any)

Dating consists of many different kinds of relationships, with a huge disparity in the level of applause. Generally you expect and hope for a certain level of approval from others, and since that does not always happen, there are not a lot of dating scenarios that we favor or are content with. We tend to get caught up with the consensus that:

Dating nobody equals being a real loser.

Very brief dating equals no substance.

Dating the unavailable equals being used.

A three-year relationship without marriage equals commitment phobia.

A long-term committed relationship equals being mature.

By negatively judging the relationship we are in, we are frequently left longing for the relationship we are not in. In our desperation to be in a favored relationship, we race ahead of what we are ready for at a particular time, and it ends in disaster, furthering the dating ordeal.

The following scenario is drawn from a number of patient/therapist interactions, and depicts how a person can disregard who and where they are in their life in terms of respecting themselves:

A woman says, "I want to be in a committed relationship."

I respond, "Your words say one thing, but your behavior says another."

"What do you mean?"

"You comment that you don't feel good about yourself and frequently tear yourself down verbally. All this negativity limits you. Why would a committed man, who accepts himself, be interested in you when you pose as someone who thinks little of herself?"

"Well, that is what I share with you. I don't tell that to others."

"How you carry yourself energetically counts. It sends a message that you devalue you and can only match up with a like-minded man in a limited relationship."

"The only problem is that I don't get to meet the right types of men because I don't go to certain places."

It is not where you are, but who you are that matters. The type of woman you see yourself as will determine the type of man you can connect with."

"It is hard for me to trust that."

"I realize that, but from that view you will just need to be content with the unavailable or limited men you tend to get involved with at present."

She protests, "I don't want that."

"It is up to you. I have no preferences. I am just mirroring what you tell me and others. We can only give you who you are and the plan that your behavior calls for. Who you can be with is reflected in the words, thoughts, and positions you take."

"You want me to be accountable for all that?"

"You can choose to or not. I can't make that choice for you."

She says, "I'll think about it."

8. The Belief That The Lover You Desire Is Lost

There is an extremely seductive word that is used in many book titles for singles. The word is FIND. Where to find your lover. How to find your lover. What is in the way of finding your lover. All of this is based on the premise that your lover is lost, and as a result you need to search anywhere and everywhere to find him or her. On top of this, the clock is ticking. Regardless of where you may believe that your lover is hiding, the search can get very exhausting and will often leave you vulnerable to chase after whatever single ads seem the most appealing. I especially was impressed with the ones for gorgeous Russian women and millionaire men.

The preponderance of this inner turmoil, frustration, and running around in circles becomes unnecessary when you are able to shift the attitudes and thinking that are creating your dating ordeal. It is not easy to do, since the mental and emotional conditioning is deeply ingrained, but the impact on your dating life will be well worth it.

Making the Paradigm Shift

All of the factors that contribute to the dating ordeal have one thing in common: hierarchical thinking. In this kind of thinking every relationship or behavior is rated as better or worse than something or someone else. Any differences we come across, fat-thin, tall-small, short-long, or intimate-shallow are used to establish this hierarchy. From this perspective we tend to focus on dating or our dates as the problem. Neither is true.

We just end up ranking everything to death, especially ourselves. It doesn't occur to us that our hierarchical thinking is the real problem.

The answer to getting beyond the dating ordeal is discovering a new way to think in which the typical judgmental dating game becomes a level playing field. To do so will require a paradigm shift from your current ways of viewing things, that is, a fundamental change in your approach or underlying assumptions. Many of the concepts I will be mentioning in this book, such as "all dates are successful" or "there are no bad dates, just dates" go against the hierarchical mental conditioning you've been subject to for many years. It will not be easy making this shift since you're used to thinking that dates are either successes or failures, and your friends have validated that perception. I liked Nina Atwood's (Be Your Own Dating Service) statement that "Successful dating is a journey, not a destination."

I will be sustaining this non-judgmental attitude throughout this book to the point that you may think that I am absurd. The reason for making no exceptions to this premise, even in regard to the notion of bad dates, is because to do so places me right back into the hierarchical thinking we are so accustomed to. My suggestion as you read through this book is to clear your mind of your usual assumptions, and consider a different way of viewing things.

A New Attitude Toward Dating

A new attitude requires a new language in order to make the shift from typical conditioned thinking. The list includes:

- Replacing rote judgment with acceptance
- Replacing rejection with permission
- Replacing feeling victimized with accountability
- Replacing drama with real excitement
- Replacing blame with respect
- Replacing impersonal with personal

The focus then moves from ranking everything as better or worse to accepting each dating experience for what it is rather than what it is not. Give yourself permission to be who you are in all of your dating relationships by making clear, accountable dating plan choices, by respecting the integrity of each dating situation, and treating yourself and others in a personal way. In doing so you will discover a new way to date and create the relationship that fits you.

I especially want to emphasize what it means to be personal rather than impersonal.

Often when you experience parts of yourself that you deem unattractive or unacceptable, you will treat them as something you'd prefer to get rid of or hide. As a result, sadness, awkwardness, inadequacy, weakness, and fear, along with other traits, are thrown into a can marked *Emotional Discards.* When this occurs, important parts of your humanity are lost, and you spend your entire dating time hoping no relationship will expose them. In addition, this activity will naturally spread to the people you date, as you carefully train the microscope on them to unearth whatever traits they may be hiding so you can reject them for it.

All this changes when you adopt a personal attitude. You will be kinder to the person you are, imperfections and all, as well as to those you meet. In the personal world we are all just people, not objects to compete with or get something from. We are merely reflections of each other, not separate aliens.

There are no Surprises

So much of the emotional turmoil and frustration that is part of the dating ordeal is due to our insistence in acting surprised by what goes on in dating, who we meet, and how things turn out. As a result, we get surprised by the testing that occurs, rejections that happen, hidden judgments, and sudden endings.

Despite what you may believe about the mysteries and unknowns of dating, there are no surprises. A great deal of what evolves is predictable if we choose to be awake to what is in front of us. The information is all there, we just ignore it for whatever reason.

A prime goal of this book is for you to develop a perspective on your dating journey that will allow you to say, "I knew exactly what was going to happen with dating him, and the resulting relationship didn't alter my perception one bit."

There is No Drama

Dating doesn't have to be a drama. It only becomes a drama when we judge and object to the many experiences that emerge in the dating process. When you learn to accept the nature of dating, the dating scene can become playful and fun rather than a living drama.

From the judgmental perspective this is not possible. But remember, we are now shifting our thinking.

What if we reversed the entire acceptance-rejection drama, and instead of objecting to what we consider the limitations of dating, we allowed ourselves to enjoy them? What if we laughed about, and even played with, our concerns, instead of grimly resisting them?

Can you picture having fun with the possibility of rejection? Can you visualize the relief you would feel if you and your date decided to relax and share many of the feelings and concerns you had been carefully hiding from each other?

Imagine this scenario: You and your date get together, but instead of the usual superficial, polite exchanges, you get right to the heart of the matter – will you accept or reject the other? You each know "judgment day" is coming, so why not deal with it openly and honestly right up front. You ask each other, "When can I count on you rejecting me?" Forget the disclaimers, such as, "Who knows when that will happen?"

Let's say your date answers, "After about three months, I'll probably start giving you mixed messages followed by a comment like, "This relationship doesn't feel right to me."

Instead of going into the typical, "I'll feel rejected" spiel, you might retort, "Tell me in detail how you plan to pull this off. Lay out the whole setup and the drop-off." Almost in shock at this invitation, your date rattles off a scenario he has never told another living person. For example, "After the first month my eyes will start wandering, and I'll become less interested in what you're saying. I'll also begin to show up late or miss dates altogether with somewhat respectable excuses. "Fascinated with this openness, the potential rejectee forgets that she might be the object of the rejection, and becomes intrigued with the drama—almost like watching a play. Then in the spirit of this openness and lightness, you can share the ways in which you will probably reject him, so you can complete the mutual rejection dance.

After thoroughly enjoying the expose', you both now have a fair and reasonable choice. Either you can thank your date for the entertainment, or you can choose to be a character in the other's play, but now fully aware of the possible outcome. If you choose the latter, you can make announcements as the relationship progresses: "Sixty days to the big rejection, thirty days…"

I once saw a commercial that blatantly exposed the judgmental dating scene. A man comes to the door to pick up the girl, and as soon as she opens the door he says, "Gee, I expected you to be cuter." Without hesitation she says, "I thought you'd be more mature looking." Sensing his style, she followed that comment with, "Are you sure you are ambitious enough to go out with me?" He says, "I've got nothing better to do."

In another encounter, this on the series *Once and Again*, a woman runs into a man who looks familiar:

She: We've met before

He: No, we haven't. I'd have remembered.

She: Obviously you didn't, because we have.

He: Oh, yes, now I remember. I thought you were a snob.

She: And I thought you were a jerk.

He: Well, why don't you give me your phone number again.

She: What for? I don't want you to call.

He: It doesn't matter, since I wasn't really intending to call anyway.

While this kind of an exchange might horrify some people, I loved how refreshing and freeing it was. Typical dating doesn't come close to this kind of openness.

There are no Bad Dates

Consistent and essential to leveling the dating field is to accept that there are no bad dates; there are just dates. Stay with me here – I can almost hear the protests: "Are you nuts? You just haven't met some of the turkeys I've been out with. I am a genius for picking out the creeps." I'm not talking about situations in which your physical safety is threatened. As with everything else, you have to use common sense when you are out there dating. Always take steps to protect yourself from harm, especially with complete strangers who you meet on the internet. Aside from these instances, as I stated previously, if I make an exception and refer to the existence of bad dates, I will be right back into the hierarchical thinking which consumes our culture.

The thinking that bad dates exist is based on three positions:

- Clinging to the vision of being attracted to only certain dates.
- Failing to ask the question "Who is this date bad for?"
- Unwilling to accept what the date sitting in front of you is offering.

All of us have a vision as to what is a good date and what is a bad date. What we fail to realize is that this perception is entirely subjective. There is no one definition of bad.

To some people "nice" is bad, while to others "rough" is bad. No characteristic is left out of the good-bad continuum. Even things you would think are positive like being "direct," can end up in the bad pile. I recall one woman sharing with me that she couldn't stand this guy. I questioned, "What was so bad?" She said, "I didn't like how direct he was about everything. It made me feel naked."

Since anything can be labeled as bad, we need to concern ourselves more with who is this date bad for. As you will see as you go through the various dating plans, anyone can be bad for a particular plan. A needy woman will be seen as obnoxious to a brief dater, while the same woman is heaven to a rescuer. Ultimately, unless we look at bad in terms of context and match-ups, it has no meaning.

When you remove the label "bad," let go of your attachments in the moment, and accept what your date is presenting, you can come to see that dates run the full range of human experience. This perspective allows you to become fascinated with the various types, play with them, and even learn from them. How much time you spend with any one dating experience is up to you, but I guarantee if you see your dates in this way, you will no longer feel victimized.

You may ask how this is possible when your date is not just unpleasant, but even rude and obnoxious. A man who talks loudly, curses, and tells crude jokes would certainly be viewed as a bad date to be dumped as quickly as possible. But you have another choice.

You can let go of your attachment to being polite and respectful, accept what is happening, and then, with a straight face and an inquiring tone say, "So, are you always this rude, or is your behavior especially designed for me?" Or, "I'm curious. If you weren't trying to be on your best behavior and you were to give yourself complete freedom to be totally obnoxious, what would you do?" I assure you, if you can pull this off with a straight face, your whole evening could turn around, and you could start to have fun with whatever your date says in response.

Here's another instance. On the first date, your date spends the entire time talking about his sexual conquests. Most women would be turned off by this. However, when it happened to Janine, she asked him, "Is there a woman you have slept with that you haven't told me about?" The question startled him. Without halting for a second, she pressed on, "Now, exactly which of your conquests do you consider the most impressive?" Not prepared for any woman to be this direct, he began to change the subject. By taking control of the situation instead of withdrawing or making feeble objections, Janine ended the evening feeling her own power. She was pleased that she could walk away without feeling victimized by another so-called bad date.

As a result of the ways we rank everyone, it is hard to consider that the so-called bad dates we run into offer anything to learn about ourselves. Consider the case of Cindy who, over the period of a month, had been chatting on the phone with a man she'd never seen. Comfortable that he'd passed the phone test, she looked forward to the date they had arranged. He wanted sushi, and they met at a well-known and expensive restaurant.

During the meal they ate and drank heartily. Their total bill was $150. She offered to pay half, but he refused, which, at the time, impressed her.

Her excitement quickly faded when they walked to her car after leaving the restaurant. Within seconds he was all over her physically, and continued his aggressive advances despite her protests. Finally she broke away and drove off, while he yelled, "Chicken!" at her disappearing car.

Most men or women would regard that as a terrible first date, and I certainly don't approve of him violating her physical space, but it turned out there was much for her to learn here about how she failed to take care of herself. She had gone along on an expensive first date, drank too much, and minimized her date's failure to provide straight answers throughout the evening. Because of this experience, she will probably handle herself with more care on her next blind date.

There are no Wrong People

For those of you who have made, "Why do I always get involved with the wrong ones?" your theme song, I want to propose that nobody ever picks the wrong mate. Even our most disastrous choices are somehow the right match at a specific time. However, if you still want to cling to the illusion that you're the victim of random, accidental dating choices, be my guest. You'll get plenty of support from your friends. But you'll be missing something important.

Nina Atwood in her book *Be Your Own Dating Service* concurs with this perspective when she states, "It is too easy to brush off our past mistakes in relationships as being a simple matter of having chosen the 'wrong person.' It is much more challenging and infinitely more rewarding to look to ourselves for the source of the problem. After all, what is the common denominator of all your relationships? You are, of course."

When you acquiesce to the view of so-called wrong partners, whether you are conscious of it or not, it's because you are failing to recognize that there is something in that kind of relationship that fits who you are and what your personal agenda is at that time. As you will come to see when you read about the individual dating plans, all partners you select are a result of the plan you have chosen for that time in your life.

They are not mistakes. They reflect your core intention. In fact, they are the best person with which to carry out that plan. If your agenda is intimate safety, then a married man is not a mistake, while an available, committed man would certainly be the wrong choice, despite his positive image.

In an early episode of the TV show *Sex and the City*, Carrie, the female lead, is confronted by her therapist about why she always picks the wrong men. Carrie resists the idea that she does, saying, "I don't do that." But later in the story, Carrie makes love to one of her therapist's other clients, a man she met in the waiting room following one of her therapy sessions. Afterwards she asks her lover, "What's the problem that you're seeing the therapist about?" He answers, "I lose interest in a woman right after I make love to her." Then he asks, "Why are you in therapy?" Carrie blurts out, "I always pick the wrong man."

I believe Carrie is not with the wrong man. She instinctively found a perfect fit. It is only wrong because most people would assume that she is LTCR material. If Carrie could be more honest with herself about the kind of man she's ready for, no matter what her friends and therapist say, she might have a lot less pain. Of course, that doesn't make for good TV drama.

There are no Unsuccessful Relationships

Once you can make the shift to this new way of thinking I am proposing, you will see all your relationships differently. You will no longer be caught up in a sense of failure and have to play the, "Why do I always pick the wrong ones?" game. Instead, you will regard all your dating choices as successful relationships. One-time dates are successful one-time dates. Three-month relationships are successful as three-month relationships.

A man married three times is a successful short-term marriage selector. Any date can be successful if it matches up with your

Personal Dating Plan goals, rather than some standard offered down by consensus.

The only reason we see relationships as successes or failures is that we compare our choices to something they are not. This thinking is a giant trap. It limits your ability to engage and learn from the full range of human experience. We compare three-month relationships to long-term committed relationships. We compare unavailable people to available people. Each relationship has its own integrity and needs to be respected for what it is. Even unavailable people are available for something, such as great fantasies, when we don't view them through a one-dimensional lens.

When Renee came to see me she was quite depressed over the demise of her five-year relationship and felt that she had failed again in selecting a man whom she wasn't able to depend on. In exploring her history she revealed that her parents were totally undependable, and her whole life was built around the belief "I can only depend on myself." Upon hearing this I explained to her that her relationship was the successful expression of her core belief. It was not a failure. Her inability to create an interdependent relationship with him was consistent with her thinking, and was the motivation behind her current dating plan. It was fascinating to watch her initial attempts to twist away from the truth of this, and then see her subsequently understand the power of her belief in influencing her life.

I don't believe in merely focusing on The One as the only successful relationship, and the single people I am in contact with

35

reflect the need for an entire spectrum of relationships. Seeing relationships as The One or Not the One is too small a box for people to be in. In John O'Hanlon's book *A Guide to Inclusive Therapy*, he quotes family therapist Kevin Hardy. "Life is a messy and confusing middle ground, neither here nor there, never just black or white. It's just as important to resist the pull of polarized thinking: either/or, good or bad, or any one of the million dichotomies that shape our identities and our culture." In realizing this, then all our relationships can be seen as successful.

Your Lover Is Not Lost, You Are

It is rare among singles to find anyone who is not attending the "seeking school" of dating, yet the number who graduate is relatively small. I previously stated that the predominant thinking in this school of thought is that the mate you are seeking is lost somewhere, so you need to look all over to find him or her. But what if the lover you want is not missing and is just waiting for you to be ready? It is my perspective you are the one who is not able to see your lover or behave in a way that allows him or her to move toward you. The problem lies within your own perspective. If you claim you can't see anyone out there right now who fills the bill, it is your blindness that is the problem, not his/her invisibility.

The confusion arises because we are trained to think in terms of form, not energy. If we can't see it, it isn't there. Yet your energy has much more to do with the kind of person you are with than some idea you have about who that person should be. You can spend hours in your head wishing for Mr. or Ms. Right, but if the energy you can handle is minimal, you will attract a person who is minimal.

If you are really serious about a committed relationship, then from the perspective am proposing, you will be asked to trust that the person you have longed for is right here in front of you.

When I first saw Randy, he was going out with a half a dozen women, many of whom he had no interest in beyond friendship. He felt he was on a treadmill going nowhere and would question himself after each date as to why he even went out with the person or had sex with them. When I questioned what he wanted, he said "A committed, serious relationship." I said, "If you want that, you will need to make some changes in your thinking and your behavior." He agreed and expressed an openness to doing anything. I said, "You may have trouble with what I am going to say." He repeated his desire for something new. Yet, when I began to share with him that "The woman you say you want is right here and she has been watching and waiting for you the whole time," he retorted, "You're kidding me." I went on to say, "She will not impose herself on you because that is not the way energy works. She will merely reflect your openness and readiness to see her. When you can do that, she will manifest in your life and the search will be over."

In response to his ongoing doubts, I related that he could certainly go back to his old ways and all the relationships his mistrust has gotten him. I reminded him again that "This path will require considerably more trust than you are used to allowing." He clearly let me know that he didn't want any part of the old way, so he agreed to trust and listen further.

I told him that, "It is important for you to trust the fact that your prospective lover knows what you are doing, makes no judgments about you, and merely waits for you to get tired of your running away and avoiding her. Only you can let her in the door. The decision is yours to open the door or not. She will patiently watch and wait.

I then asked him to tell me, at present, how far away did he sense she was. In the beginning she was a 100 yards, and over time he would report her moving closer and closer. Throughout this period I would let him know each time he would change the integrity of who she was, a woman he desired and who also wanted him, by making statements such as "She won't want me or I won't want her." I constantly reminded him that she wants him and he will want her. That is her nature.

During this period his respect for himself had increased dramatically, he felt much more peaceful, and he had no interest in his old dating plans. After not seeing him for a month, he declared he had met the woman in his imagery and that I wouldn't believe where it occurred. Even I was surprised when he mentioned that it was in the garage of his apartment dwelling in which she had recently moved. Even though the relationship was relatively new, his description of the relationship and the woman had no similarity to his dates of the past.

Knowing What You're Ready For

The whole point of this book is to help you end your dating ordeals by seeing that all dating is about match-ups between people who share the same state of readiness. In my own story, approximately six months after my divorce, I was sure I wanted and was ready for another long-term committed relationship. Despite great efforts, it was not happening. All my so-called long-term dates ended up in short-term relationships, whether I ended things or my dates did. I finally had to admit I wasn't ready for a long-term committed relationship, but rather for something much more brief. A few months after admitting that truth to myself and expanding my own availability, I connected with the love of my life.

It made me reflect that a lot of people run into trouble because the kind of relationship they think they want is a stage or two ahead of them and isn't what they're really ready for. That is why they keep thinking they are ending up with the wrong person; why they find themselves extremely frustrated due to their own impatience. Many singles make this mistake, and as a result miss out on some relationships that could work well for them.

When you fail to recognize what you are ready for, you are frequently left running after and longing for an LTCR, while discounting all other dating relationships just because they don't look like LTCR material. That is why I wrote this book – to support you in your quest to become honest with yourself about the kind of dating experience you're really ready for, and to respect that as your integrity. I assure you, if finding the LTCR is your eventual goal, it will come along when you're ready for it.

The truth is, you only get the relationship you're ready for, regardless of what you say you want. What we are ready for and what we believe we are ready for are often two quite different things. Recognizing that fact can come as a great relief. Suddenly, the pressure is off and all your dating behavior begins to make sense. You will come to see that the kind of relationship you are truly ready for is actually what you will be drawn to and end up with, whether or not this is what you think you want.

Charlotte had known Jim for twelve years and had even been engaged to him twice. Each time she broke it off with some justification. He was devastated on both occasions. For the last five years, she had been in several different relationships with little satisfaction, while maintaining an every-week contact with Jim, at times by phone and occasionally in person. Recently, she decided she really wanted to be with Jim, and told him so. He was startled, and let her know that he was currently seeing someone else.

Charlotte said she understood the timing wasn't right, but she felt she still wanted to be with him, and decided just to be patient. He kept calling her and telling her he was not sure what to do with her new request, since he had been burned by her several times before.

After two weeks, Charlotte's stance that she was ready for a committed, intimate relationship and was willing to be patient, collapsed in a sea of panic, anxiety, and demands. "When is he going to decide already?" she asked herself. To hasten a decision, she phoned him several times, but the added pressure did not provide her with the answer she was looking for.

What Charlotte didn't realize was that she wasn't ready for an intimate relationship with Jim. Her impatience, demands, and excessive preoccupation indicated she was only ready for distrust and pushing someone away. If she truly wanted to connect with him, she would have to relinquish her self-righteous position that since she was ready, he should be, too, and meet him at the only true place – that neither one of them was ready to risk being committed to the other at the same time. When she did, it eliminated the anxiety she was experiencing. She found comfort in not pretending that she was anything but what she was. Whether they ever got together is not relevant. What matters most is that she had begun to respect who she was, and not simply run after her fantasies.

The key to knowing what you are ready for is determined by your ability to recognize the dating messages contained in your actual dating behavior and being responsible for those choices at a particular time of your life. Charlotte's behavior indicated a desire for an extended relationship coupled with a lot of drama and an intense fear of putting two feet totally into a relationship. Her running style and her impulsive needs for immediate gratification made accountability a questionable event. You may experience discomfort at the thought, but unless you own your dating pattern, you will be forever run by it as her situation illustrated. Learning to be accountable is the only way to change a repetitive dating pattern, because you cannot change what you don't own. That is why, with any addiction, you are asked to admit first, "I am a ..."

With that knowledge, you can never be ahead or behind yourself. If you walk no faster than all aspects of you can support, you don't leave any part of you behind in the rush to move ahead, and you will experience greater trust in yourself. Leave out any part of you, and your trust will dwindle. It is a good rule to walk at the pace of your slowest part. So if trusting a man is clearly your most reluctant part, then it would best to recognize the nature of that trait or you may send yourself in to orbit.

Marty was in the second month of a new relationship following the heartbreak and breakup with a woman who he deeply loved. A part of him was still saddened and fearful in opening up again. His lady on the other hand was ready and willing to move ahead and increase the commitment. While he cared for her he wasn't able to brush aside his fears, despite her insisting that "I am not like your old girlfriend." He was feeling a real dilemma. In this instance, I supported him to respect his fearful part and not leap over this feeling or he will regret it. He decided to follow his reluctant part openly and honestly, and it did wonders for his healing and his sense of himself in the relationship.

Another aspect of readiness is accepting what a relationship calls for – not what you wish it is, but what is the exact reality of the relationship. Richard was involved with Angela for several years, in what he called an exclusive, committed relationship. He would often express dissatisfaction about her failure to be with him more often, due to her continuing involvement with her ex-husband. It was proposed to him that the relationship wasn't offering exclusivity, but was more reflective of, "I do what I want, when I want, and with whom." Once he could accept this as the real truth, he began to date other women along with Angela, and his frustration lifted. Thus, an excellent question to ask yourself if you are also in a relationship that frustrates you is, "What involvement of mine does this relationship call for, so that I am not giving too much or too little?"

In many instances the inability to ask the most effective questions serves to cripple one's readiness to move beyond certain dating plans. Typically "why" questions such as "Why do I meet the wrong people?" "Why didn't it work out?" or "Why do I always end up with mediocre dates?" will leave you feeling like a victim and maintaining the illusion that you had nothing to do with what happened on your dates. Goodbye, accountability.

Beverly Hutchinson, a colleague of mine and a follower of the Course of Miracles, a self-study, spiritual psychotherapy, has developed a simple way of avoiding the victim trap and opening people up to a more responsible path. She believes that as long as you ask predominantly, "Why?" questions, such as those mentioned, you will remain in a continuous circle. The reason is that "Why?" promotes blame and self-accusation.

When you blame, you will need to defend. When you defend you will blame, and the circle is complete. To break that repetitive cycle, a much more beneficial question is "What for?" which alludes more to the purpose of your actions. "What did I meet that person for?" "What did it turn out that way for?" "What do I always meet these kinds of people for?"

Notice that the "What for?" question takes your eyes off the other person. Rather than judging others as wrong, bad, or mediocre, it invites you to look at yourself. From this perspective, all of these questions will lead you toward learning about yourself, regardless of what happens on your dates, and help you raise your awareness of yourself.

In this way there is something for you in every date, rather than seeing all dates as either good or bad. The perception of your date as wrong is transformed into seeing the particular lesson you need to learn.

Julie, a sensitive, timid soul went out with a man who was aggressive and loud. She was upset initially with how bad she felt on dates with him because of his extremely loud voice. She questioned, "Why do I run into these kinds of men?" In switching her question to "What for?" it became apparent in a short time that she had been running away from men of that kind all her life, and had never been able to take care of herself when she was around them. She also remembered that her father, whom she loved, acted the same way. She had been running, not away, but toward the remembrance of the only father/daughter love she knew by drawing these kind of men to her.

Sooner or later you may ask, "How can I know when I am ready for more?" You'll know when you start longing for someone different and begin losing interest in the relationships you have been involved in. As your level of emotional, mental, and spiritual readiness expands, so will the kinds of dating plans you'll be ready for.

Everyone has a Personal Dating Plan

A Personal Dating Plan rests on your recognition and pursuit of the plan and partner that is the best match for you at a specific time in your dating life, a relationship you can emotionally support. The task ahead is to decide what you can handle, then determine what kind of man or woman best matches your current requirements. Remember, this has nothing to do with what you think you should aspire to eventually, that LTCR perhaps, because that's a whole different story. Each plan is acceptable as long as it fits you.

None is regarded as better.

Once you know what you can support emotionally, you can select from any of the fifteen types of dating plans suggested in this book — dates with ambivalent or emotionally unavailable mates, dates with addicted mates, dates with geographically undesirable mates, dates with psychologically crippled mates, dates with financially impoverished mates, or dates with passive or controlling mates.

While many of these types are rarely on anybody's LTCR list, they may be perfect for you right now. If they match what you can support emotionally, date them and enjoy them. They can teach you a lot. In some cases, what they'll teach you is that you want more than they can offer, and in others, that you need to remain with them a while.

An "A" for Courage

In spite of all the dating war stories, I've come to see daters as courageous souls who deserve a lot of respect. The woman or man who reaches out to someone unknown and agrees to spend time with them is taking a risk. You have to admire them for that. Both sexes struggle with the process of dating and all it demands, but if they view it as part of their dating journey, they will see any difficulties as opportunities for them to learn about themselves.

By developing this attitude and the new way of thinking presented here, the dating road ahead of you will become less of an ordeal. Just remember:

- There are no surprises
- All dates are the result of our choices
- Everyone we date is right for us at a certain time in our lives
- There are no bad dates.
- All dates offer something
- All dates are successful in that they are just what they are meant to be
- All dates can be fun when we can enjoy the integrity of each dating experience.

From this viewpoint, you won't need to defend any of the relationships you are involved in. Knowing you are in control of your destiny and not a victim of random choices can also help you stop dating in the dark, and start dancing in the light. You'll actually enjoy dating. It will no longer seem like such an ordeal.

Now, let's take a closer look at what you need to do to prepare yourself for selecting your Personal Dating Plan.

PART II

THE NEW DATING PERSPECTIVE

CHAPTER 2

THE PERSONAL DATING PLAN

Date: *To go on a date, to take out, accompany, escort, court, woo*

Plan: *A method devised for making or doing something or attaining an end, blueprint, design, game plan, project, scheme, strategy.*

Merriam-Webster's Collegiate Dictionary

Many dating books help you find ways to manipulate others in order to get the partner you want. You are advised to: Say this, do that, wait on this, hold back on that – all designed to help you get The One. I have no interest in joining that parade. In fact, this book is not about telling you how to behave in order to get The One. It is not geared for one particular way of dating, nor one goal. Rather, its purpose is to help you better understand and benefit from your entire dating journey wherever it is at a given time.

The Personal Dating Plan concept allows you to go beyond prescribed ways for you to be, because it's geared just for you. Nor is your dating plan something you are supposed to keep secret from your dates. In fact, I recommend that you share it with your dates so you will be dating honestly and on a level playing field.

It may surprise you to know that you already have a Personal Dating Plan. You probably think that all you've been doing is muddling through, hoping things will work out for the best, and not really understanding why they're not. But, as you will soon see, no matter what you've been up to, it's still considered a Personal Dating Plan, and you are its sole creator. Nina Atwood, *Be Your own Dating Service*, says, "How we date is how we relate. The two cannot be separated." Thus, whatever way you relate is your Personal Dating Plan, regardless if your are conscious of it.

Dating In The Light

The key to making your Personal Dating Plan work for you is to learn to date consciously. Conscious dating means being aware of the plan you are in, knowing the goals involved and the choices that play into it, understanding how your dating plan serves you, being accountable for your choice, and sharing your thoughts and feelings about it with your partner in a direct way. Conscious dating asks both you and your partner to show up without your facades so you can give and receive honest feedback while providing a mirror for the other. Honest feedback is not merely saying popular or expected things, but stating where you are, whether it seems unacceptable or not. Does that sound like a tall order? It is, which is why so little dating is done consciously.

Initially, most people relate unconsciously. Unconscious dating is the antithesis of conscious dating. In unconscious dating you muddle through essentially clueless about the messages you are sending out to the dating universe, have little or no awareness of the Personal Dating Plan you are into, act seemingly confused over why you pick the people you pick, and in the end feel quite puzzled and often disliking the results. Unconscious daters typically act shocked and surprised when their own or their partner's behavior doesn't match up to expectations. "I didn't know he was married!" "She didn't tell me she could only see me twice a month."

In conscious dating there are no surprises. Daters know what they are picking and why, and they know the consequences that go with the territory. Pick an alcoholic, and no surprise when she drinks to excess. Pick a married partner, and no surprise when he spends holidays with his family. Pick a withdrawn man, and no surprise when conversation is minimal. Pick an angry woman, and no surprise when you get dumped on.

The whole game of playing dumb and then acting like a victim will become history as you become a conscious dater. When you are conscious of what's actually happening on your dates, you'll encounter fewer surprises and be far more relaxed.

As you consciously own your plan and you are more willing to attest to this being your choice ("I do three-month relationships and prefer it that way.") with all its consequences, your consciousness will increase even more. The last step in conscious dating is to decide when the plan you have been doing no longer fits you, and you are ready to support a different plan. "I have done brief relationships and now I want to be in a long-term, fully-committed relationship."

The 15 Personal Dating Plans I'll be discussing in this book are:

1. The *Date Nobody* Dating Plan

2. The *On-the-Clock* Dating Plan

3. The *I'm a Seeker* Dating Plan

4. The *Comfort Zone* Dating Plan

5. The *Status and Conquest* Dating Plan

6. The *High Drama* Dating Plan

7. The *I'm Available to the Unavailable* Dating Plan

8. The *Parent/Child* Dating Plan

9. The *Rescuer/Savior* Dating Plan

10. The *I Get Ahead of Myself* Dating Plan

11. The *It's Time I Got Married* Dating Plan

12. The *I Need a Father/Mother for the Children* Dating Plan

13. The *We're Worlds Apart* Dating Plan

14. The *Extended Relationship* Dating Plan

15. The *Long-Term Committed Relationship (LTCR)* Dating Plan

As you'll see, some of these dating plans overlap others, so primarily you want to focus on the one that fits you best. Keep in mind that no dating plan is better than any other. This may be hard to grasp at first because we're all so conditioned to ranking and judging relationships as better, healthier, and more mature than others. What really matters is that your Personal Dating Plan reflects your own truth at a particular time in your life, taking into consideration your relationship anxieties and fears.

Who Am I and What Do I Need Right Now?

But before you head off looking for the dating plan that matches up to your needs, answer the questions below so you can get a better idea of what kind of person you are right now and what kind of partner you are capable of connecting with at this time. The partner you may be looking for down the road is a whole different issue. Our focus is on the Dating Plan which fits you *right now*

1. What's your track record?

Looking at what you've actually been doing is your best clue to what dating plan is right for you. For example, you may think that your dating has been about looking for that LTCR (marriage, settling down, etc.), but is it? Your real dating plan shows up in what you're picking, not in what you're wishing. If a woman says she wants a committed relationship but she keeps dating married men, then her real dating plan is safe relationships with men who aren't available to her full-time. If a man says he wants a trusting relationship with a good woman but he keeps picking angry, chaotic, disloyal women, then the truth is that his real dating plan is intense, chaotic, roller-coaster relationships.

Look at your dating choices over the past year or two. What do you see there?

Then look at the list of 15 dating plans and select the one that most resembles what you've actually been doing. In determining the plan that fits where you are, you need to also consider what kinds of partners go with that particular Personal Dating Plan.

Providers are only interested in little girls. Rescuers prefer cripples. If you don't have enough perspective on yourself to answer these questions, ask a good friend who will be honest with you, "What kind of Personal Dating Plan do *you* think I'm into?" Don't bite off their head if you don't like the answer. Just ask yourself if what they are saying is true, and does the dating plan they see match what you are emotionally and mentally supporting.

I recommend that at this stage you stick with the dating plan you can support, and don't try to move on to another dating plan too quickly. It doesn't matter if the relationship you are into lasts for three dates, three months, or three years. Only take on what you can handle at the moment.

2. What are your priorities?

This is an important question because it will reveal the bottom line of many of your relationships. For example, if work is your number one priority, if your heart belongs to the office or to some time-consuming creative passion, then all your protests about wanting a deep love relationship do not hold water. Your priorities will dictate what you can emotionally support and provide realistic clues to your partner as to what they can expect from you.

Priorities may include such things as career, family, friends, hobbies, making money, time alone, or travel. Later in this book you'll read about relationship priorities that include safety, excitement, sex, power, and variety.

Your own personal and relationship priorities are going to influence the kind of dating plan you'll be available for. If you are divorced and your children are your number one priority, you may only be able to support a *Date Nobody* dating plan (Chapter 3) or an *On-the-Clock* dating plan consisting of brief relationships (Chapter 4). On the other hand, if safety is your number one concern, then The *Comfort Zone* dating plan (Chapter 6) or *I'm Available to the Unavailable* dating plan (Chapter 9) may be your ticket.

3. Can you "own" your current dating choice?

This is a step that many people skip over. You might think, "All right, I see that I select unavailable men, so I'll change that and select available ones." The problem is you have never really assumed ownership or accountability for the old plan, and now you are merely saying what sounds good, which only continues to cloud the issue. This will not solve anything. Instead, once you figure out what your current dating plan is, be honest with yourself and own it 100%. Initially, it will be difficult. You will probably feel like objecting vehemently, or think, "OK, I accept it, but I don't like it." However, accountability is only reflected in the statement, "I do it, I accept it, and I like it!"

In addition, you need to be willing to share the truth about your dating plan with others without any hedging. If your dating plan is a string of three-month relationships, so be it. Be accountable for that. Say, "I only stay in relationships for three months. I like the turnover. I like getting out before things get too complicated." If someone gives you a hard time about it or tries to put a negative label on you ("You can't commit.") learn to respond in a non-defensive way. Say calmly, "You may not care for it, but it suits me."

4. What is your love capacity?

Everyone wants to be loved. Most singles devote themselves to looking for that love.

Yet it is probably rare for any of them to ask themselves, "What is my capacity to receive love from another person?" It is erroneous to assume all of us are fully open to receive love just because it is offered to us. Each person has a specific capacity for love that is limited by fears, beliefs, past wounds, and familiar circumstances. If all these factors combined only allow us to be loved halfway then our love capacity would be 50%. Any attempt to create a relationship that requires a greater love, such as a long-term committed relationship, wouldn't work; we would be unavailable for it.

Each of the dating plans mentioned in this book asks for different love capacities. *Dating Nobody* asks nothing, brief dating asks minimal amounts, extended relationships asks much more, and *Long-Term Committed Relationships* asks the most. In becoming aware of which plan is most suited to you, it is vital that you have a clear understanding of your own love capacity. Failure to do so will create a lot of inner turmoil as well as frequent conflict with others who expect more than your capacity to receive.

Nadine was confused about why she seemed to reject men who were very caring and loving, and was drawn instead to angry, distant men. Once she revealed her history of feeling unloved and distrustful, it became clear that her ability to receive love was very limited. When Nadine was with men who were loving, those limits were exposed, but with angry men she didn't have to face her own deficits.

Carolyn was depressed about seeing so many of her friends in committed relationships when she was still alone. I asked her, "What are some of your beliefs that make this outcome impossible for you?" At first she said there weren't any, but when I asked the question again, she admitted, "I can't allow any man to know about my past because I'm ashamed of it, and I don't believe any man I would like could be interested in me."

The point is not for everyone to be fully open to being loved by another, but for each person to honor the integrity of her/his own limits. A capacity of 50% is not bad; it is just 50%. Knowing your capacity provides a starting point from which you can increase your capacity to receive love if that is your goal.

To help you determine your love capacity, imagine a scale of 1 to 10, with 10 being the highest capacity. Rate yourself accordingly and use that number as your capacity.

As you encounter different dating experiences, you can adjust that number if it seems high or low.

5. How does your current dating plan serve you?

Daters tend to judge their current dating plan situation negatively, especially if they think others might devalue or disapprove of it. They think *Dating Nobody* is bad, and *Dating the Unavailable* is worse, and not being ready to move up the dating scale is something to hide. Despite these common judgments, all dating plans serve a purpose and have a positive intention. Every plan, regardless of what it is, has benefits and consequences, an upside and a downside, just like everything else in life. Dating nobody provides time to focus on other things in your life, just as dating the unavailable allows for safe intimacy. The true spirit of the Personal Dating Plan approach is that there are no negative, bad, or wrong dating plans. There are just dating plans to take care of your primary needs of the moment. Your job as a dater is to weigh the upside against the downside of each dating plan, and make the dating choice which best serves you.

6. What are your dating "red flags"?

Red flags are deal breakers. They are warning signs or danger signals that let you know a particular person could end up not fitting into your dating plan, resulting in eventual hurt or disappointment. Red flags appear in many forms: a one-line remark, a sudden look, or a bit of behavior that reveals the core truth about a person. In one case, a woman was out on a date with a man who tossed out a remark that the Holocaust never happened. At the time she didn't give this comment a lot of attention. It was not until later that she realized his view reflected a righteous, closed attitude that led to the end of the relationship.

On a first date you need to watch and listen carefully for these red flags. They may only last a few seconds, but will stand out in sharp contrast to the charming image the person you have just met is trying to paint of himself or the relationship he proposes.

Red flags can alert you to any future relationship conflicts, as well as problems that may arise at some point during this date, or subsequent encounters.

Here are a few examples:

- A man says that his whole world is his work and his kids. That's a clue that in the dating show, you'll be backstage.
- A woman states that she doesn't know what she wants from a relationship. That's a warning that she'll be equally ambivalent about you.

Many times singles are so busy trying to make a good impression, or feel so needy, they discount or are oblivious to red flags from their date. Afterward they are puzzled about what finally emerged in their relationships. Cari was dating Rob for about four months and starting to get serious when the relationship collapsed in the face of his immature behavior. She had earlier seen a fairly rosy picture. When pressed to remember any red flags, Cari revealed that when she told

Rob she sees a therapist, he became quite arrogant and said, "I wouldn't go to one, no matter what." That was a clue to all the self-important behavior and lack of openness that followed later, but at the time she minimized it. If Cari's dating plan had been to go on a few dates and quickly end it, Rob's attitude wouldn't have mattered, but for her plan, it should have been a neon sign flashing "Beware!"

It is generally agreed that red flags go up for someone who is unemployed, very self-centered, or on record as preferring non-monogamous relationships. I don't agree. In my opinion, there are no universal red flags. The only red flags are those behaviors or intentions that will interfere with your needs and Personal Dating Plan goals.

In fact, any red flag will have quite varied effects on different people. What might make one person run for the hills may have no impact at all on another. So while Cari's date's objection to therapy was a giant red flag for her wanting a committed intimate relationship, I have come across several women who prefer a man that is closed to therapy. They prefer to stay within their safe walls and don't want any man learning things which would enable him to see through these barriers and expose her.

You discover your new acquaintance is married. Is that a red flag? Well, if you're interested in a safe relationship with plenty of time off and few demands, you will want an unavailable partner because that is all you can emotionally support at the time.

Whereas, if you found someone who wants to marry you, it would interfere with your dating plan goal of staying separate. Conversely, if it's an LTCR you're after, "married" isn't going to do it for you.

Even a man who is actually willing and available for an intimate relationship can raise a red flag for some women. One woman met a terrific man she felt she could easily fall in love with. The problem was she had just started dating after her divorce, and wanted to do what she had never done before – date a lot of men. Being with an emotionally available man she could care about was a definite negative for her dating plan.

What about dating men on death row? Most would venture to say that's a definite red flag. Why, then, do some women do it? If playing the excitement game while avoiding everyday intimacy is all they can support, there is no problem. It's exactly what they are ready for. It matches their Personal Dating Plan perfectly.

7. Are you singing one tune and dancing another?

Maybe what you wish you were doing, or think you should be doing, isn't what you actually are doing. There's a disconnect going on. The words and the movements don't match. You insist you're looking for one kind of relationship, but you keep ending up with another.

Denise, a 34-year-old woman, complains that she meets a lot of great men, but none of the relationships work out. Why would this happen? Because in each relationship she makes a determination about what the man wants, and then tries to give it to him, meanwhile hiding her own needs and opinions. As a result she ends up clueless about who the men really are. Afraid to rock the boat, she doesn't ask any real questions that might get her dates to reveal anything truthful about themselves. Instead, the men just do whatever their typical act is. And since she always defers to them, they in turn don't see who she really is. In the end, she gets to act surprised by the way things turn out, when in truth she orchestrated the whole thing. The men just go along for the ride as long as it meets some of their needs.

So how do you account for the discrepancy between your words and your behavior?

The rule of thumb is to assume that your behavior is the truth and the other stuff is just a wish. When you violate this rule, you will send yourself spinning. If your body says, "tight" and your words say "open", you can assume you are guarded. If your words say you are secure, but your behavior says you are running, assume you are insecure.

An excellent exercise to determine your behavioral dating position is to ask yourself frequently, "Where are my feet pointing?" It geographically illustrates where you are in your current relationship. Look and see if both pairs of feet, your own and your date's, point toward the relationship, away from it or are split. If your feet are pointing toward the relationship and your partner's feet are pointing toward and away, it will have a tremendous bearing on the attitude displayed in your dating. Your relationship will be a study in ambivalence, and back-door escape routes will be open to different degrees.

Nancy, a forty-year-old female, had been struggling with her boyfriend's reluctance to make a commitment. She was always trying to get him to do more in the relationship, and he'd respond with an assortment of vague excuses about why he wasn't ready yet.

She needed to recognize that her boyfriend had only one foot in the relationship. His feet made clear where he was at, so all her energy to change it was useless. When she was finally able to accept his true relationship stance, she was able to walk away. Nancy could have saved herself a lot of pain if she'd been able to recognize and accept the position of his feet earlier.

I mentioned this concept to another woman who was also constantly focused on changing her boyfriend. I reminded her that since she, herself, had only one foot in and one foot out in her relationship, there was no point in questioning him on his commitment. When she finally shared her own position with him, it cut down on their arguments and debates dramatically.

8. What do you find scary in relationships?

Relationships are the great humblers; they expose us to the hilt. It's uncomfortable to have to look at our powerlessness, helplessness, imperfections, limitations, and vulnerabilities. Whatever is unknown to you in your relationship experience will reveal your core fears. If you haven't dated at all, even a beginning date will be unnerving. If you tend to be a pleaser in your relationships, then expressing displeasure over something, or standing up for yourself will terrify you. Imperfection will scare you if looking good is your main concern.

The truth is, everyone is afraid in relationships – and that includes your partner. It's just that different people hide their fears in different ways, and some have more deceptive acts. First and foremost, be wary of any man or woman who tells you he or she has no fears about a relationship. One man said he had no fears in regard to his wife, yet he presented an extremely protected self. Almost everything he said to her was designed to prove or defend something. No one exhibits this kind of behavior unless they are very frightened.

To help you discover the nature of your fears and your partner's, look for what seems missing from the picture you each paint. If either you or your dates presents yourselves as a study in perfection, you can bet that the sight of any imperfection is the greatest fear. If a hatred of weakness is mentioned, write it down as the biggest fear.

Let's say that the person you are considering hates it when he or she feels helpless in the relationship. If you choose to be with a person who fears helplessness, be prepared to have them insist on helping you, but when you try to help them, expect to hear, "No thanks, I can do it myself." Their need is to protect their image of not needing help.

As an additional word of caution, don't accept your date's answers as to what they fear where you are the focus of their fears.

67

Protesting, "I'm afraid of our relationship ending," is just surface smoke. Any real fear was present long before you arrived on the scene and is much deeper.

What about the love so many say we dream of and desire? That is one of the scariest experiences of all. Because many of us went through our early years feeling unloved in some way, we are not prepared to receive love in an intimate relationship. Thus we often pick partners who are not able to give us such love. In that way we don't have to worry about receiving love, and we can remain within our comfort zone. If you want to leave your comfort zone, you will need to admit, "I am afraid of anyone really loving me."

Admitting you are afraid, and what you are afraid of, will allow you to be less defensive in your relationships, no matter what dating plan you select. You don't need to protect what you are open about. Throughout this book I will return to this idea again and again, and I will be asking one key question: *Are you willing to be afraid, or are you stuck in being afraid to be afraid?*

The idea of allowing yourself to be afraid goes against our cultural conditioning. We have been taught to attempt to get rid of our fears, as they are perceived as obstacles that inhibit our free action. Nothing could be further from the truth. Fear of being afraid is what limits us, not fear itself. The more willing you are to let yourself be scared, the better your chances of getting the relationship you want. This is essential if you are considering an LTCR.

How you deal with your relationship fears will determine what dating plan you select and will affect your capacity to move from one dating plan to another. Each single person I work with who desires a new plan with greater relationship demands than the present one, I ask the question "Are you willing to be afraid?" Anything short of a clear YES I consider to be merely lip service.

I frequently refer my single clients to the movie Defending Your Life in order to illustrate the importance of a person's willingness to be afraid. In this movie Albert Brooks is killed and ends up in Judgment City. In Judgment City he goes before a tribunal who possesses every scene of his life. The tribunal is prepared to make the decision whether he is to be sent back to Earth where he will continue to use 3% of his brain, or be allowed to move on where he will use 45 % of his brain. Their sole criteria is based on looking at his life and concluding whether he has learned to be comfortable with fear or does he continue to run and hide from fear. It is difficult to watch this film and not ask the question of yourself.

9. Are you really ready to change?

At some point you will ask yourself if you are still satisfied with your current Personal Dating Plan or are you ready to move on. Your plan may have served you well up to this point, but is it still offering you what you need in your life? If not, it may be time for you to choose a different one. When you do, remember to pick only a plan you can emotionally support, otherwise you won't be able to deal with the results.

Merely getting outside pressure to change your Personal Dating Plan is not a good reason for doing so. If you are ambivalent about moving on, hold off. Your ambivalence is telling you something. You will thank yourself many times over if you follow the rule to interpret all ambivalence, your own and somebody else's, as a "No." I have seen many people move ahead, disregarding their ambivalence, and ending up extremely frustrated down the road. It is respectful for you to admit to yourself in the face of your ambivalence that you are not ready to give up your old dating plan at this particular time because it basically still fits who you are.

Here's a paradox for you. You will be ready to change your current dating plan only when you can accept your current one and "own" it 100%, with no judgments or emotional reactions. Attempts to change before that happens will result in false starts because you will unconsciously be communicating two messages: *I accept/ I do not accept* my current dating plan.

Consider the situation of a man who felt pressured to date when he really didn't want to. He knew he couldn't support it emotionally. When asked what kind of relationship he thought he could support, he said, "I do best e-mailing. I may phone a girl from time to time, but I won't sound real interested or have much to say. If I ask a girl to meet me, I can never come up with a place because I figure she won't like it. If we settle on a place to meet, I won't say much, won't even appear interested. I may look like I'm having an awful time because I have already decided that I am not good enough for her or anyone else. I may ask a few questions, but I won't reveal anything about myself. When it's all over, I won't ask the girl out a second time, and we'll never see each other again."

This young man's Personal Dating Plan could be called the *Date Nobody* Dating Plan.

When I told him that, he laughed, and even seemed relieved. It legitimized the stage he was at and where he needed to be for now. I recommended that he hook up with some on-line chat rooms and be up front that he didn't want to date. For the first time in years he stopped beating himself up for what he saw as his limitations. By owning up to his Personal Dating Plan, he set the stage to move forward.

Like this young man, one day you will arrive at a place where you will be able to declare to yourself, and to the world, that you are ready to move on to a new Personal Dating Plan and to someone who can fit into this new plan. A woman whose Personal Dating Plan has been going out with unavailable men may now be ready for a man who will make her number one, a man she will not have to share with someone else. Or a man may realize he wants a woman who is independent and can stand on her own, rather than choosing women who are victims in life, and then trying to be their rescuer. When you have truly reached this stage, you will be able to support this new level of relationship 100%, just as you were able to support the dating plan that came before it.

Four Dating Plan Variables to Consider

Within each of the fifteen Personal Dating Plans, there are four variables to consider that can influence how you experience that dating plan.

Variable #1: Awareness Blocks

The ability to recognize your own dating plans and be accountable for them is crucial in forming your entire dating perspective. Anything that gets in the way of your awareness will greatly limit your learning ability when you are sincerely choosing to consciously date. There are several blocks that need to be addressed in order to decrease that possibility and stay clearly on your chosen dating track.

The idealization fade

While dating, a part of you may want to stay in a euphoric state, blissed-out because you have at last met the person who has everything and possesses no flaws. This idealization needs to be recognized for what it is – an illusion. Otherwise, prepare yourself for the full illusion crash alert that happens when the image of the date you fell in love with begins to fade, and the other's true character shows up. Some daters feel betrayed by this occurrence and spend extensive time trying to get the other person to recreate the face they fell in love with.

Julie had recently fallen in love with a man who seemed understanding, accepting, and loving. He came from a background where everything was neat and everything had its proper place. She liked the fact that he had this kind of order in his life. In the beginning they dated only on weekends, and predominantly on his controlled turf where he was most relaxed and comfortable. However, as they began to spend more time together in a variety of settings, everything started to turn. She began to see that he got irritated and angry over the slightest thing that didn't go right. She felt very uneasy as her fantasy began to show cracks, and sad that she might have to see who he really was. Every time you choose to idealize your dates rather than seeing them for who they are, your ability to date consciously will be diminished. You need to choose if you prefer the blindness of your fantasies or living with your feet on the ground.

Hitting your wall

Sometimes the situation you blame for not allowing yourself to attain relationship goals is not the real problem. In fact, it is the exact opposite, and if you don't come to realize this, you end up looking in the wrong direction and feel totally surprised while getting ambushed from behind. You need to be looking out for whatever things are unknown and unfamiliar in your life, because this is where you will find your wall. If you find you are worried about anything you have experienced many times over, you are fooling yourself. A true wall cannot be anything that is familiar and known. If you have had many experiences of failure, this is not your major concern. Sooner look in the direction of allowing success in your life as your real wall.

After a sixth date, Laura was feeling extremely nervous about her relatively new relationship. She had been through a number of prior relationships and had experienced plenty of rough patches, but this one was going far too well! She was convinced that something was going to go wrong and she would lose him. She began to create mental scenarios of herself as inferior, even though he had not given her any indication of this being so. Still, she could not shake the fear that he was going to reject her. When questioned about it, she admitted that she had never been in a relationship with a man who treated her so well. "Most of the men I've gone with have treated me like shit," she admitted ruefully. "If that's true," I told her, "why would rejection scare you? You're used to it." She had never considered that, and shortly thereafter she came to realize that what really scared her was acceptance and being loved, because she had no experience with that kind of relationship.

Too close

It is ironic that the closeness so many strive for can become an obstacle to seeing. Yet time and again, two people meet, fall in love, and end up constantly fighting. Frequently, one or both partners will accuse the other of becoming distant and not being able to stand the closeness. But that is seldom the case. The real problem is that these couples are too close. And because they are, every movement their partner makes affects them. "He didn't call. I'm so depressed." "She wasn't attentive to me at the party. I am furious."

Barbara and Bill were such a couple. There was instant attraction, whirlwind romance, and roller coaster crash. Any time one expressed any moodiness or disappointment, the other became unglued. They were, in fact, so close they were dependent on each other's every breath. They needed to understand that reacting emotionally over every nuance and behavior of the other was an indication of being too close, and every interaction comes as a surprise. Similarly, if you need the other to change his/her behavior, you are also too close. Getting closer than you can support distorts your experience of your date and interferes with your ability to make clear decisions. As a consequence you may cut off a relationship unnecessarily.

Variable #2: The Little Boy/Little Girl – Man/Woman Continuum

All of us present ourselves in one of three roles. Males will show up as passive, hiding little boys, puffed-up little boys, or as men. Females will show up as timid little girls, inflamed little girls, or as women. When you learn to pay close attention to these styles, you will more easily understand who you are dating. Both passive and puffed-up little boys are self-protective, reactive, and defended, and will attempt to prove their pseudo power by hiding or emotionally and mentally putting the other down. The man, on the other hand, has nothing to defend or prove, willing to reveal himself, and is active, not reactive. The man will stand up for all that he is, insecure or secure, powerful or powerless, honest or dishonest. When you tell a man he is insecure, he will simply say, "Yes, that's true." In contrast, if you say that to one of the little boys, the hider will withdraw into a corner, and the puffed-up will show you how wrong you are. When it comes to the little girls, the timid ones will shrink away from any confrontation, while the inflamed ones will declare war against almost any male expression through accusations and emotional barrages. The grown woman, like her male counterpart, has nothing to prove or defend. She is receptive to the man she chooses to be with. She is comfortable with surrendering, with no thought that she will lose her identity in the process. She will treat even those males she has no personal interest in with dignity and respect.

The little boy/little girl and man/woman attitudes will show up in how each person addresses his dating plan. Every dating plan will be expressed through one of these three postures, and this will affect the nature of the participant's dating behavior. Both little boys/little girls and men/women do brief dating, but there is a world of difference in the experience. Little boys and girls will assume a defensive posture in regard to a brief dating plan and will sneak in and out of the relationship. A man or woman doing brief dating will be upfront about it, noting that if it doesn't work well for the partner, he/she will accept that.

When a timid little girl does *Dating Nobody,* she will say dating is too risky and scary. The puffed-up little boy who is into the same plan will say that no women are equal to him so there's no reason to waste his time. Real men and real women, on the other hand, say flat out they are into *Dating Nobody* because they have other priorities. They do not see it as a problem, nor do they need to justify it or blame anyone for it.

In order to help people make these distinctions, I recommend the visually stunning and poetic movie Dangerous Beauty which takes place in 15th Century Venice. The female lead truly models the characteristics of a feminine woman who has nothing to prove and has the courage to surrender, and it also shows several of the males transform from puffed up little boys into men.

Variable #3: The Four Levels of Relationship Agreements

Dating is all about making agreements. Every dating plan starts with an agreement, with additional agreements being made along the way, from dealing with the simple issue of meeting again to the deeper, more complicated issues of sex and marriage, and everything in between. The moment you ask someone out, you have made an agreement.

I agree to see you on this date at this time and in this place, and we agree to engage in some kind of activity such as coffee, a movie, or dinner. From that point on there is a continuous river of agreements. Do we agree to go out a second time? A third time?

What are we going to do on those occasions? Do we agree on when to be sexual? Are we in agreement as to what this relationship is and where we are going with our dating?

The one thing you can count on is that many of the agreements you make will be sloppy, partial, or vague. That's because we all have different ideas about what constitutes an agreement, and some of us aren't willing to make the commitment that is necessary to create solid agreements. We go around thinking that a partial "yes" or "no" is a real agreement. Some assume that a "maybe" is a "yes," while others hear it as a "no." And how many times has this happened to you – your date says he'll call and you never hear from him again? Or you tell your date you'll see him again, but when he calls to confirm, you leave the answering machine on and don't pick up. Experiences like these make you think that maybe you need a hearing aid or a refresher English class. It's no wonder that so-called agreements can lead to distrust and frustration.

If you are considering dating someone for any length of time, you need to be clear about which of the four levels of relationship you're saying "yes" to –the mental, emotional, physical, or spiritual. In this context "spiritual" has nothing to do with religion, but rather relates to your higher purposes. You may agree to have a relationship on only one of the four levels, or on all four. If you agree that all you want from each other is a physical relationship, then the rest of it doesn't matter. If you want only a challenging intellectual relationship, then the emotional, physical, and spiritual aspects are most likely irrelevant. If you want an LTCR, then it is best that you get a "yes" on all four levels or you're going to experience conflict down the road. As long as you both truly understand what you are there for, and agree, you are a good match. But if one of you wants a physical relationship and the other doesn't, that will become a constant source of frustration.

Jeannie had been through a series of unstable relationships. She started going out with Bart, who had an established career, made good money, and seemed extremely stable in the way he handled his life. This made her comfortable both mentally and physically. Emotionally she experienced a very different story. He left her feeling unexcited and flat.

She tried to tell herself that she would learn to feel more, and that stability was more important. Despite her mental efforts, the relationship faded after a few more attempts, as her lack of a "yes" on the emotional level became more and more apparent.

Differences in interest that occur in many dating relationships bring the issue of agreement to the forefront. While dating would certainly be less difficult if all rejection was mutual, that is frequently not the case. One of you will be riding off alone as the other one calls, "Come on back! Let's give it one more try." Sometimes the dates you reject will drown you in compliments, persuasive monologues, and outright demands in an effort to change your mind. Those who are still not convinced will come up with cute phrases like,

"We could really be great together." "We have so much in common." "Your parents will like me."

Indications that your initial interest is not being sustained occurs when waves of boredom begin and you experience a significant strain in keeping up the conversation.

Once you have exhausted typical questions and answers, if there isn't some emotional or intellectual interest, you will be left with gaps of silence. Then you must decide whether to stand up for your lack of agreement in interest in the relationship, or soft pedal it.

Marie, a 24-year-old with average looks, was dating Robert, a 28-year-old attorney. When she told him she found him too materialistic and wasn't interested in seeing him again, he turned up the juice. He blurted out that he thought she was one of the most beautiful girls he had dated, and he loved looking at her. He added in no uncertain words that she was making a big mistake in rejecting someone who appreciated her so much. While Marie felt all right about herself, she was not used to a man coming on this strong about her looks. She could feel herself start to doubt her original judgments and begin to buy into the thought, "How can I leave someone who adores me this much? "Maybe I have been hasty." Her mental body was clearly setting off her emotional feelings. It took some strength to get out the door and never look back. Once she was able to get some distance from the extremely seductive comments, she again returned to trusting her original opinion.

It takes work and perceptiveness to listen to our dates and ourselves on all four levels in order to get what each relationship story is about. I recommend that you ask the four questions with each of your agreements. For example:

- Do I have a mental "yes" for going out with this person again?
- Do I have an emotional "yes" for going out with this person again?
- Do I have a physical "yes" for going out with this person again?
- Do I have a spiritual "yes" for going out with this person again?

By doing so you will get a much clearer understanding of just what it is that you and your date are agreeing to. Perhaps you are agreeing to go out as just friends. If so, it would be helpful knowing that up front and not at the end of the evening.

Variable #4: Everyone is a Package, Not a Chinese Menu

In choosing a mate for your Personal Dating Plan, you need to realize that each person you select is a package deal. You don't get to pick one part from Column A and one from Column B, as if you were in a Chinese restaurant. If you choose that person, you get the whole menu.

One client shared with me that the man she had been involved with was a great guy when he wasn't drinking. When I asked how that resonated with her, she quickly replied, "Well, if he was no longer drinking, we could have a beautiful future." I responded, "So what you have is a great guy alcoholic." She didn't like hearing the combination and tried again to split the two parts. Each time she did this I repeated, "He is a package deal. Do you want the package?" After several rounds she said, "No, if you put it that way."

You can save yourself a lot of aggravation in selecting partners for your plan if you ask yourself the question, "Do I want to be involved intimately at length, or even briefly, with this person's package? Yes or no?" This is true even with very brief sexual relationships. Knowing the emotional instability of a particular woman, a man still chose to have sex with her. After being dragged through a legal process by her, defending a variety of allegations, he admitted that it was the most expensive sex he ever had. He could have avoided it by asking himself at the outset, "Do I want this package?" rather than relying strictly on his physical body.

Foreplan

I'm not a great proponent of "shoulds" in relationships – you should get married, you should share, you should/shouldn't have sex without commitment, etc. I prefer that people learn to guide themselves and base their dating plan choices on who they are, not what somebody else thinks they should or shouldn't do. I have two simple rules. In selecting a dating plan, don't go any further than you can emotionally support. Don't do any more than a relationship asks for. If you are a weight lifter and can support and carry 250 pounds, fine. If you can only carry and support 25 pounds, don't try for more and risk hurting yourself.

In the dating plans you'll find described in the following chapters, you will discover a strong emphasis placed on you, the reader, rather than on the variety of lovers you may run into. The descriptions will speak mostly to your intentions and motives, rather than your date's. Your dates will be treated as merely reflections of your intent toward the particular dating plan you favor. This shift of focus will have a direct impact on how accountable you care to be in regard to your dating life.

Remembering the Dating Plan Basics

Before you rush off looking for a mate, it is important to keep in mind certain criteria in the selection of your Personal Dating Plan.

- Pick dates that match your Personal Dating Plan. For example, "I prefer married men since they can only demand so much from me, and I can obsess about them in total safety."

- Live your plan at the level that it is, not more or less. For example, if it is just friends, then stay within those boundaries and don't go beyond that.

- Respect your current love capacity. "My negative beliefs don't allow someone to truly love me.

- Be accountable for your Personal Dating Plan. For example, "I like dating three people at the same time, and I understand all the consequences that go with that plan."

- Accept your dating plan without judgment. For example, dating nobody is not a bad thing or a problem. It is one possible plan with its own integrity.

- Be positive about your Personal Dating Plan and embrace it 100%. For example, "My friends are disapproving about my choice to date married men, but I totally accept this preference in my life at this time."

That said, let's get to the substance of this book – the fifteen Personal Dating Plans.

PART III

THE DATING PLANS

CHAPTER 3

THE *DATE NOBODY* DATING PLAN

If you're not dating at all right now, you'll assume you don't have a dating plan. But opting not to date is also a dating plan, in that it has its own set of rules and presents a specific course of action.

Dating nobody means you have to make sure that nobody asks you out or tries to fix you up. If they do, you have to make sure you say no. If you doubt this requires effort and discipline, try imagining what it takes to *not* have any dates for a year or two.

It takes work – even though the idea that doing nothing takes energy may sound strange.

But think about it. Every day that you go out into the world you need to consciously push people away, avoid eye contact, and make sure you keep all your inner and outer doors closed. People who favor this plan need to be dedicated about it. It's not a plan they can practice only on Tuesdays. It's a 24/7 job, with no holidays or time off.

At a recent gathering, a young woman admitted she practiced the *Date Nobody* Dating Plan. Immediately, ten or twelve people surrounded her in an effort to convince her to date, and that her concerns about dating were unfounded. She brushed aside each attempt, explaining why dating wouldn't work for her. In the end, her dating plan remained intact, her resolve unshaken.

There are several ways to guarantee you will date nobody. You can maintain an isolated existence or hang out in groups so nobody ever gets to see you alone. But in the latter case you will be exposing yourself to more people, and if one of them is highly motivated, he/she may attempt to cut you away from the herd. Another way is to maintain an exaggerated sense of self-sufficiency and self-reliance. Convince yourself that you don't need anybody except yourself. Still another method is to practice self-ridicule: "I'm fat, ugly, unsuccessful, and undesirable. "That's always a good way to ward off prospective daters so you can successfully uphold your *Date Nobody* Dating Plan and avoid being hurt at all costs. Here, of course, you need to be careful that some other "ugly, undesirable" person doesn't end up regarding you as a soul mate.

The primary focus of the *Date Nobody* Dating Plan is rejection, and the fear of it guides your dating life. To put yourself in a position where you might be rejected is seen as a fate almost worse than death. As one woman stated, "If I let someone reject me, they'll share what happened with others, and soon everyone will know, and I will be totally humiliated."

By not giving anyone the chance to reject you, you are not exposed to the awful feelings which you believe go with that territory. This was certainly the case with Sandy, 18, who wanted to make sure no fellow ever had the opportunity to reject her. For Her, the *Date Nobody* Dating Plan was ideal. Despite numerous offers from friends to help her meet eligible males, she begged off. On one occasion there was a dance in which the girls were to ask the boys, but she still refused to participate. If she happened to be in the presence of a boy she liked, she would dip her head so they could not make eye contact.

However, the plan works just as well if you do the rejecting. You can hold onto such thoughts as: "There are no men for me, all the good ones are taken," or, "All the men in this town are superficial." These can be extremely effective in sustaining your commitment to the *Date Nobody* Dating Plan.

There are some single people who advocate the *Date Nobody* Dating Plan, yet attend singles events as observers. They'll stand on the sidelines and entertain themselves by labeling all the men as creeps (or all the woman as dogs), thereby justifying their decision to date nobody. This way there is absolutely no chance they'll weaken by being in a place with so much potential, since there isn't going to be anyone suitable to date.

The *Date Nobody* Dating Plan is all about safety and self-reliance. No vulnerable part of you is exposed, and no one gets to see what you are afraid of, sad about, or ashamed of.

The threat of self-revelation is avoided when there is no one around to see the real you.

When you choose the *Date Nobody* Dating Plan, there is no one for you to need, no one to take care of you, and no one but yourself to depend on. You alone are the person who will have to fulfill your needs for love, security, food and entertainment. You are it.

This can be hard to handle at first, but ultimately you are bound to find many creative ways to take care of yourself and build your self-reliance.

John, 48, was an avid practitioner of the *Date Nobody* Dating Plan. His devotion to the plan was amazing. He had built an entire world in his one-bedroom apartment. His place was filled wall to wall with his solo projects, one of which was the collecting and selling of old CDs, and he spent all his hours amid the clutter. He hadn't had a date in ten years. His decision to avoid dating stemmed from two humiliating experiences with women during his early years, and was designed so that no one would ever hurt him again. In therapy, when he finally became willing to look at the fact that his whole life had been built on a belief he made as a young man tying hurt and shame together, he said, "I can't believe I haven't moved beyond age seventeen."

Ned, a 50-year-old gay man, was a master at manifesting halfway relationships. He was so good at it that it was unclear if he and his partner were actually dating, and if they were, where it was going or what either of them wanted. He referred to their meetings as "hanging out." In that way no one needed to commit to anything, and the relationship could last for years. Yet he would not accept that he was accountable for this choice, and claimed to want something more than a halfway relationship. To help him become more accountable, I suggested he give a personal name to his halfway plan. He came up with "Nebulous Nibbler". The name amused him and served to make him more consciously aware of his behavior. Taking more responsibility for his choice energized him, and soon after, he left the half-way plan behind him and started to date actively.

Tron, a young, good looking, and highly intelligent law student with a great many talents, was far from a genius when it came to reaching out to women. His ongoing mental litany was, "She'll turn me down. What will people say if I date someone at my law school? She's not good enough for me. What if it doesn't work out?" The only woman he reached out to was someone who already had a boyfriend, as the chance of anything happening there was slim to none. Through therapy he became aware that he had managed to believe the fictions he created in his head about why he couldn't date.

Like so many people who subscribe to the *Date Nobody* Dating Plan, he had a very involved relationship with himself, and reacted to all his internal chatter as if it were real.

The "If" School of Dating

Tron, like so many other people who swear by the *Date Nobody* Dating Plan, was reluctant to own it. He didn't want to appear uncool or foolish, so he fabricated a little story to save face. He told others that if the right girl came along, he would be open to seeing her. But, of course, the right one hadn't come along. "You wouldn't want me to become involved with just anyone, would you?" he'd ask. This allowed him to date nobody and look good doing it.

We live in a couple's world where choosing to be alone is suspect. If you follow the *Date Nobody* Dating Plan, expect to be viewed as having a problem, or dismissed as a neurotic, a misfit, or a nerd. When you are around friends and family, you'll get a lot of advice: "Try dating," they'll tell you. "Take a risk, it won't hurt you. I have somebody I'd like you to meet." Rarely will others simply be willing to accept your decision to follow the *Date Nobody* Dating Plan without question.

<u>Rules of the *Date Nobody* Dating Plan</u>

- Avoid dating at all costs
- Tell yourself that dating is awful and rejection will be devastating
- Talk only to friends who support your negative view of dating.

Who to Play With

- Nobody
- Anyone who would never ask you out
- Anyone you'd never consider going out with

The Upside of this Dating Plan

- You'll be safe from any rejection or failure
- You'll learn to depend only on yourself for everything
- You'll feel great pride in your ability to be alone

The Downside of this Dating Plan

- Your life will seem very familiar from one year to the next
- Lots of people will offer you advice
- Others will look at you as if something is wrong with you
- Life will be the sound of one hand clapping

The Dynamics of the *Date Nobody* Dating Plan

Low self-esteem and a strong negative belief system can be what attracts one to the *Date Nobody* Dating Plan and keeps them stuck there. Usually, the person grabbing on to this plan has had some kind of powerful, humiliating, or traumatic experience early on, and even now considers any kind of re-exposure to the feelings involved as tantamount to emotional death. These people usually operate from their emotions rather than from a strong, logical base. Since they have built an entire identity around negative thinking, they fear that their personality structure would collapse if this plan were to be violated, a circumstance much worse than simply not having a date. In summary, those who select the *Date Nobody* Dating Plan are usually strongly committed to it and believe they are justified in choosing this plan. They need to accept that's where they are and stay with this plan until they are ready to move to another one.

CHAPTER 4

THE *ON THE CLOCK* DATING PLAN

You're ready to date, but you don't want to fall into what you see as a Venus Fly Trap where you'd be subject to the demands and expectations of a relationship. You have no interest in staying around that long. You're "on the clock," so to speak, and will soon feel the need to move on.

There are two kinds of people who gravitate toward the *On the Clock* Dating Plan.

The first group consists of those who need to go through a period of having many dates with many people. For example, a person who, after very limited dating, married young and then divorced, would find it helpful and interesting to do a lot of dating in order to gain more experience and discover what he/she does and does not like. A lot of short relationships would permit that. This used to be referred to as "sowing your wild oats, "and if you haven't gotten that out of the way, it could result in a wandering eye and a lot of fantasizing about others once you're in a committed relationship.

Mary had been married for five years to her high school boyfriend. He was the only man she had been with sexually – in fact, the only man she had ever dated. When they got a divorce Mary jumped right into another exclusive relationship. While this served to relieve her of some of her insecurity and loneliness, she felt guilty because she found herself fantasizing about other men. When her boyfriend accused her of being distant and preoccupied, she told him she was tired or busy with work. However, as the relationship continued, it was clear there was more to it than that; she had entered a committed Dating Plan prematurely. This dating plan choice was not a good match for this stage in her life, and she needed to first date a lot of men.

The second group of *On the Clock* daters don't view this dating plan as a stage to pass through, but as a place to stay. They want to date "on the clock" all the time. They like the many benefits this plan offers, especially the opportunity to keep starting over fresh with a new person so they never have to feel stuck or bored.

Devotees of the *On the Clock* Dating Plan have different timeframes they are comfortable with before moving on to a new person. Some select one month, others three months, while others may like to hang in there for as long as six months. Only you can determine what length of time fits you. Here's where you have to be sensitive to what your internal clock is telling you. If you leave too soon, or hang around too long, you'll become uncomfortable.

Those who favor the *On the Clock* Dating Plan seem to have their watch in one hand and their car keys in the other. When the alarm goes off, it's, "Gee, is it three months already? Time to move on. Hasta la vista, baby!"

Single people who support this plan typically love beginnings. They love the excitement of a fresh, new relationship when everyone is on their best behavior.

During this early period no one wants to make demands or even let the other know what their expectations are. So it is an easy time for one and all, which is fine for those who prefer brief dating.

When this fantasy ebbs and the relationship begins to get a little messy, a whole different story unfolds. Now there are questions about being on time, why didn't you call, and is that the extent of your openness? *On the Clock* daters abhor discomfort in any form and take it as proof that they were correct in not wanting a long-term relationship.

The more unaware followers of this plan will act surprised when it is revealed to them that relationships carry expectations. Others know that demands will be coming but hope they can extend the ride for a while until that occurs. They use discomfort as a barometer to alert themselves to when the end may be drawing near, and then they back off.

When Tom was 25, he would meet a woman and jump into a relationship that for the first month was hot and heavy. By the second month, things would begin to cool off and he'd see the woman with less enthusiasm. She'd begin to complain that he was changing. By the third month, it would become obvious that things weren't the same anymore, so by the end of that month the relationship would just fade away. Tom might have saved himself a lot of drama and aggravation if he'd just been up front about his *On the Clock* Dating Plan. "I only see women for three months and then I prefer we go our separate ways. I don't do more than that. So if you would like a short ride with some exciting moments, then let's get it on. Time's a-wasting."

Proponents of this plan need to be clear that the person they are dating is not The One. It doesn't take a rocket scientist to know that if you want to limit the relationship, you had better not get attached to this person. Not being tied is your key to leaving. Otherwise, you will find yourself devastated.

Some people who date *On the Clock* share their dating plan openly, but most do not. If you crave the initial excitement of new partners, you obviously wouldn't want to throw cold water on a prospective date by showing your intentions. Also, by allowing the partner to think the relationship is more than it is, you get the pleasure of seeing it heat up fast. Since the burnout will be equally fast, the primary goal of keeping the relationship short will be attained. Usually, the end game will appear to be just an unfortunate occurrence on the dating pathway, rather than it all being part of a specific dating plan from the outset.

This plan works best with people who don't take care of themselves in the beginning by expressing their needs or asking pointed questions. In contrast, if you choose someone who insists on the relationship not moving fast or is concerned about not getting ahead of himself, it will become difficult for you to reach your burnout goal. It's also hard to put this dating plan in action if your partner asks you from the beginning how long your relationships usually last, or why you want to move so fast.

In order to make sure you are choosing the right people for brief dating, you might consider the following questions:

- Are you and your date comfortable with limited commitments?
- Are you and your date fairly content with your own independent lives?
- Are you and your date willing not to need each other?
- Are you and your date willing to experience other lovers?
- Are you and your date able to resist falling in love?

Since the fear of the unknown bothers many of us, the openly *On the Clock* dater benefits by taking that element out of the equation. You know going in approximately how long this relationship will last, despite what you may both be telling each other in the heat of the moment. With the unknown taken care of, you can feel liberated, knowing that your ticket out of there has already been purchased.

There is probably no other plan that offers you such a variety of relationships. You can have involvements with at least six or seven partners a year and look forward to more the following year. Sarah was seeing three men concurrently, as none of them would see her more than once a month. One lived in another town, and the other two claimed to be too busy. For some women this would be unacceptable, and initially Sarah complained that the men didn't give her enough time. But when she was willing to be honest with herself, she realized that's how she preferred it. She wasn't ready for more. The *On the Clock* Dating Plan allowed her to space out her dates without having them conflict with any of her many other interests.

As with other dating plans, this also has an unattractive flip side. While the *On the Clock* dater gets to start new relationships continuously, it's easy to get drained by all the new beginnings. Your inner voice may moan, "Oh, no, not another person I have to go through the getting-to-know-you routine with. I'll say *this*, and then she'll say *that*.

All predictable, all boring!" Then there is self-chatter about whether you'll make the right impression, how long to date, should you have sex or not, etc., etc., ad nauseum.

And the inner dialogue goes on and on.

No matter what questions run through the *On the Clock* dater's head, there will always be a sense of "I've been there before," and a weariness due to the fact that there is rarely depth in these relationships, so you will not have the opportunity to discover the deeper aspects of one another or see each other in various situations. However, for those who don't like exposure and the development of tighter bonds, this will not be a loss.

Over time most *On the Clock* daters start to feel a longing for more. When the longing outweighs the merits of this dating plan, it may be time to consider one of the other dating plans. Until then, just enjoy.

Rules of the *On the Clock* Dating Plan

- Hold to your personal time frame, no matter what
- Decide going in that this is not The One, but don't share this
- Move quickly in the beginning so the relationship burns out fast.
- Make up whatever excuses you need to break if off when time's up

Who to Play With

- Those who have similar timeframes
- Those who don't stand up for their own needs
- Those who are willing to bend to your lead
- Those who don't ask pointed questions

<u>Upside of this Dating Plan</u>

- Takes the unknown out of dating – the end is always in sight
- Get to experience lots of people in a short time

<u>Downside of this Dating Plan</u>

- Dating can eventually feel repetitious
- AIDS and other sexually transmitted diseases
- No depth, so dating gets boring

Dynamics of the *On the Clock* Dating Plan

On the Clock daters are typically individuals who prefer to avoid dealing with their sadness, depression, emptiness, and boredom by seeking distractions. They like bringing new things and fresh stimuli into their lives. Their belief is that as long as they can maintain excitement, they can avoid feeling these unacceptable and painful feelings.

A parade of new dating partners certainly serves the purpose – at least for a while.

In addition, they may also have felt that in the past they weren't able to satisfy the expectations of others, which led them to the belief that they aren't good enough. The last thing they want is to wake up every day and see disappointment in their partner's eyes, so it's best to move on down the line.

CHAPTER 5

THE *I'M A SEEKER* DATING PLAN

In Singleland, there's a lot of talk about finding The One. Where to go, when to go there, and what to do once you get there in order to make sure you find the Right One is what most dating is all about. How can you guarantee that the magic will happen to you?

The problem with this emphasis on finding The One is that the seeking part becomes more important than the finding part. If the millions of singles who are now busy seeking actually found someone, the bottom would drop out of the dating market. For some, seeking rather than finding has become the unconscious goal. These people are the ones most likely to gravitate to the *I'm a Seeker* Dating Plan.

Seeking is part of our culture, hard-wired into our human spirit. If you say you really want love, but spend all your energy seeking and spinning your wheels because you aren't finding anyone, then *I'm a*

Seeker is probably your dating plan. It may be that you actually enjoy seeking. Secretly, you're not into finding. This is a legitimate dating plan you can choose to follow like any of the rest.

One idea that propels the seeker dater is the perception that the perfect partner is hiding or scarce, so it will take a quest to find him. That means working extra hard to track him or her down, go to every singles experience in town, never turn down a party or blind date, make it a habit to case every room you're in, from the dentist's office to the supermarket on the off-chance that he or she will be there.

The determination not to miss out on any singles opportunities can be exhausting, which explains the recent popularity of such phenomena as Speed Dating. Speed Dating involves meeting at a coffee shop with about fourteen people attending. You sit at a small table and get to talk to a person of the opposite sex for seven minutes. At the end of that time you decide if you want to meet that person for a date. If there is a match, the man is given the woman's number to call at the end of the evening. If there is no match, no number is given out. Then everyone switches tables and the procedure starts all over again.

The Seeker and the Sought

In the book *The Two Step: The Dance Toward Intimacy* by Eileen McCann (Grove Press, 1987) the person that the seeker seeks is called the "sought." The sought is a person who is always moving away from the seeker, providing the seeker with the opportunity to chase after him/her. The sought is usually a master of illusiveness, a type you may have run into on your dating path. But what could be better for a confirmed seeker than someone who moves back every time the seeker moves forward? It's an endless game that works to keep the seeker stuck in place instead of moving on. It's the basis of the *I'm a Seeker* Dating Plan.

Dawn met William at a bar. At first he came on strongly. She was impressed with how articulate and confident he was, and her interest rose. They began dating. But as soon as Dawn expressed a desire to see more of William, he backed off in a variety of ways. After a while, not getting what she wanted, Dawn began to lose interest in William. When he saw what was happening, he suddenly experienced renewed interest in her. This recharged her interest again, but within days he was emotionally off again to places unknown. Their dance continued for several more sequences. In the end Dawn was no closer to William than she had been in the beginning, and she was left still seeking, hoping to find the Right One. Yet as long as seeking is her plan, she will run into many "soughts" and maintain the illusion that she really wants more.

The benefit of the *I'm a Seeker* Dating Plan is that you always have something to strive for. You are forever motivated to seek, a kind of quest for the Holy Grail. This plan also offers you an opportunity to share the frustrations of your seeking with other single travelers who will empathize with you about the difficulties and pains of the seeking journey. They've been there themselves and have a story to tell that will probably top yours.

If emotional stability is your goal, you probably won't like the consequences of this dating plan – too many highs and lows. One minute your fantasies will supply you with great elation when you think you have found The One, only to be followed by the depths of despair when your fantasy turns out to be just that – a fantasy.

Jane and Herb were active participants of singles events. Both had run the gamut of singles groups, had done Speed Dating in every part of town, used various dating websites, and had even signed up with dating services. Yet they each considered all of these experiences failures.

The pursuits were not failures, they were simply the road seekers take–people who love seeking and know deep down that no sustained relationship could happen to them.

So they kept searching far and wide for their hidden lovers, convinced they were destined to a lifetime of loneliness and despair if they were not successful. Both were also prone to blame the dating pool. "I wouldn't have to search so hard if more good people were available." Their social networks reinforced the negative view that the dating situation was hopeless, furthering the possibility of endless desperation but not fathoming a world without seeking.

Most supporters of the *I'm a Seeker* Dating Plan are loath to admit, even to themselves, that they have no real intention of creating a deep relationship with anyone. After all, they are seekers, not finders. They wouldn't know what to do with a real relationship if it came up and knocked on their front door. Chances are they'd slip out the back as quickly as possible and head right for the next singles event.

Rules of the *I'm a Seeker* Dating Plan

- Put out tremendous effort in seeking the right partner
- Go to every singles experience you hear about
- Tell yourself that the partner you're seeking is hiding and needs to be found
- Secretly doubt that you will ever find The One

Who to Play With

- Those who like to be sought
- Those who avoid intimacy
- Those who only give lip service to wanting a more committed relationship

Upside of this Dating Plan

- Always gives you something to strive for
- Serves as a motivator
- You get to go to a lot of events and have a lot of experiences
- You get to do a lot of commiserating with those in the same boat

Downside of this Dating Plan

- Periodic frustration and depression
- Always on the lookout, never relaxed
- Future, rather than present oriented

Dynamics of the *I'm a Seeker* Dating Plan

The person who is a likely participant in this plan has been damaged in the trust department. They may have experienced a lot of disappointment in early life when they counted on people, such as parents, who failed them. As a result, they carry some very strong negative beliefs about relationships. "Men can't be trusted." "Women will let you down." "Nothing comes easy in life." "If someone does come, they'll probably be the wrong one." These beliefs keep the seeker from trusting or depending on anyone, but reinforces the seeking behavior since it is preferable to dying alone.

CHAPTER 6

 THE *COMFORT ZONE* DATING PLAN

There are many versions of this plan, but they all share a common theme: maintaining the status quo and staying within one's familiar comfort zone – that place which is known and predictable. Comfort zone behavior can pop up in any of the fifteen dating plans whenever daters get stuck at a point where it's comfortable, rather than moving on to where it's uncomfortable. One such couple were engaged for thirteen years.

The *Comfort Zone* Dating Plan is popular among those who feel they have been hurt in the past and don't want it to happen again, as well as those who don't want to be exposed to anyone else's expectations. They are happy to date, and date regularly, as long as it doesn't push them from the known to the unknown, and make them feel vulnerable. To maintain this plan you need to remind yourself constantly of the dangers of going over the comfort line.

The dating that goes on in the *Comfort Zone* Dating Plan is more pretense than substance. These folks are so guarded, so self-protective, and basically so proud of how self-sufficient they are, that they might as well be dating themselves. They just bring someone along for the ride to complete the dating picture and to keep themselves from knowing the truth. Things get sticky only when their date begins asking questions like, "What are we doing here? You don't seem to have much interest in me, or want any intimate sex, or seem to care about me. What's going on?"

Good Beginnings

In spite of beginnings that show promise and excitement, the relationships of a *Comfort Zone* dater quickly fall into a pattern of familiarity and sameness, rarely progressing beyond a certain point. *Comfort Zone* daters are more interested in safety than they are in happiness. Happiness can be lost, but safety is forever, so *Comfort Zone* daters most always opt for safety.

A *Comfort Zone* dater's self-talk typically focuses on fear. He tells himself, "You'll get swallowed up." "You'll lose your identity." "You'll get hurt or disappointed." "You'll be betrayed."

As with *On the Clock* daters, *Comfort Zone* daters may choose to date only for specific lengths of time – three weeks, three months, six months. Here the focus isn't on how much time they spend with one partner, but on how comfortable they are during that time. When discomfort sets in, usually when a partner presses them for more, they get the signal to split. Dialogue exchanges between comfort zoners and their partners may include such phrases as, "Where are we going with this?" or "What's the plan?" These will be countered with, "Let's just be friends," "Why don't we just hang out" or "Why can't you just be satisfied with what we have?"

A favorite way that they attempt to protect themselves is to masterfully send their partners two messages so they cover all bases. I marveled listening to a man, who was committed to this plan, tell a woman that he was interested in dating her, but he wasn't sure that he was interested in the relationship, and this all occurred in one evening. If the woman doesn't understand the nature of this plan, she will be leaving this scene quite confused.

The main benefit of the *Comfort Zone* Dating Plan is protection of the status quo. The plan allows you to look like you are dating successfully, even though you may be stuck in the rut of familiarity and predictability. The familiarity may include no sexual involvement, no commitment, or any other static state. The only thing that matters is that it be a known place to the participants and to commit to staying there. If either pushes past this point, the whole thing collapses.

Living a life without risk, staying on familiar ground, doing only predictable things takes its toll on a relationship. After many months of this diet, the dater and/or the partner may feel empty and experience a longing for more. They may feel like passengers on a cruise ship that never leaves port. They may talk about moving on, but at the same time the love affair with the safety of this arrangement is too attractive. So instead, they endlessly talk and talk about moving on.

Tamika had been dating and sleeping with a man for five years. Yet despite the length of time, he kept insisting they weren't dating, they were only friends. When she accused him of not respecting her, he said, "What do you think I am, your boyfriend?"

Mike and Victoria had a pattern of fighting which kept them at an acceptable and comfortable distance from each other. Whenever they began to get close, they'd start a conflict over something, questioning each other about why they were even in this relationship. Eventually they began to work hard at avoiding arguments so they could let themselves experience more intimacy. That worked well until one day when they got into the very sensitive issue of Mike's eating addiction. Suddenly the air crackled with tension and emotion. This was merely another example of how they'd use arguments to avoid the discomfort of intimacy. Within minutes they were back to their old, familiar verbal attacks. Their fragile closeness quickly became a memory.

Commitment Phobics

Males who select the *Comfort Zone* Dating Plan may find themselves being labeled "unable to commit." This label is more often put on men than women, and there have been a number of books written about it, such as *Men Who Can't Love by* Steven Carter and

Cold Feet: Why Men Don't Commit by S. Rhodes. Somehow, it is assumed that women don't have an issue in this area. But many women are also commitment phobic.

They simply come up with better-looking acts to disguise it. In typical intimacy dances, the one who is moving toward the partner appears to be more open to intimacy. Many times this is not true; it is just positioning. If you look closely, you will see that the women in these cases only move forward when the man is moving away. The real intimacy test is what you do when someone is reaching out toward you.

The Rules of the *Comfort Zone* Dating Plan

- Never go outside your comfort zone
- Treat the unknown as the forbidden zone
- Regard opening yourself to another as a clear and present danger
- Tell yourself that you could be open if the other was different
- Don't trust that you are with the right person

Who to Play With

- People who insist on receiving more than you desire to give
- People who refuse to hear your message
- People who provide you with justification for not going further
- People who can't admit they are afraid of being afraid

The Upside of this Dating Plan

- Provides safety and protection
- You get to be right
- Allows you to treat your vulnerability as off limits
- Helps you justify the dangers of exposing or opening yourself to another
- Lets you tell yourself that you would be open if the right person came along

The Downside of this Dating Plan

- You will never feel you are with the right person
- You will have a deep, unfulfilled longing for more
- You will be stuck in a familiar, known, and predictable place
- You will live life without risk, and thus merely adjust and survive

The Dynamics of the *Comfort Zone* Dating Plan

Comfort Zone daters are afraid of being uncomfortable. They are also afraid of being afraid and need to protect themselves from that possibility. In the past, their parents may have strongly modeled this for them in some form, letting them know that being afraid of something simply wasn't acceptable and must be avoided. The Comfort Zoner may present an elaborate and presentable justification to cover up this truth, such as, "I need to complete my dream before I can go any further in this relationship." It is difficult to argue with that stance. To sum it up, there's something about what's being offered or suggested or requested that makes the *Comfort Zone* dater – uncomfortable.

CHAPTER 7

👍 THE *STATUS AND CONQUEST* 👍
DATING PLAN

Many of us want to feel we are desirable and seen as having status. We only differ in the manner in which we choose to achieve these goals. Typically, for a male, status comes through sexual conquest, financial achievement, and social, political, or business power. For some women it might be pairing up with someone who is powerful or who provides them with material gains.

Singles who prefer the *Status and Conquest* Dating Plan are typically ruled by their egos and use dating as a way to enhance their image. They are only interested in being with partners who serve that specific purpose. It's the ultimate *me* trip: "I want you to think I'm a great lover." "I want you to make *me* appear successful." "I want you to look up to *me* and admire *my* looks, *my* knowledge, *my* skills." The unwritten rule is that your partner is never to do anything that might deflate your image or she (the partner is usually the woman)

117

will risk facing your disapproval in the form of withdrawal, hostility, or silence. Within this plan you will find the typical male who just wants to have sex, and each sexual encounter becomes a notch on his validation belt. He will often know how many women he has slept with, their names, and attributes. He can be quite persuasive as to why you should participate in his ego quest, and will use whatever works to accomplish the goal.

The *Status and Conquest* Dating Plan works best if only one of the partners values status. That way one will be the receiver of the accolades, and the other will be the provider of the applause, the latter being someone who is comfortable looking up to, and is satisfied just being associated with such a highly desirable person. In contrast, with two people wanting status, things can get very competitive.

The beauty of this plan is that hidden insecurities are never exposed. Sex is a great distracter, and in a good match the partner will provide plenty of applause. Every morning you can wake up, look in the mirror, and feel how great you are.

The problem is the applause needs to keep coming, so you must replace any partner who doesn't satisfactorily fill that role, otherwise you are going to feel deflated and disillusioned when the approbations cease. The partners of *Status and Conquest* daters usually keep their mouths shut, but pick up more than the others realize. "He's such a little baby," said one woman about her *Status and Conquest* partner. This plan can become a roller coaster ride when the partners begin to reveal what they really think and are no longer willing to play.

Sometimes the *Status and Conquest* dater keeps another partner in reserve in case there is a drop-off of admiration.

Perhaps the most difficult aspect for those who use this plan is that the desire to be desired is insatiable and can never actually be satisfied by another, only by the person himself. In many dating scenarios, when a woman acknowledges to a man that he is desirable and she wants him, he may quickly lose interest in her. Women who find this puzzling fail to understand the insatiable nature of their partner's desire. He unconsciously needs to secure the desire of women who *don't* want him, or risk feeling undesirable. It is clearly a plan with no end, but one that many men prefer.

Constantly moving on to the next woman was not part of Pete's plan. He preferred exclusivity, satisfying his need for desirability with one woman. Pete had been seeing Sally about six months, but they were struggling in their relationship because she was only having sex with him once a day. While many would consider this level of sexual activity quite impressive, it fell well short of Pete's plan and didn't give him the validation he sought. He wanted Sally to have sex with him three times a day. These demands left Sally feeling like a machine, not a woman, and she said so. Pete interpreted her remarks as meaning she did not care about his desires, and he was not important enough to her.

Their arguments on this subject would go on and on, as none of the reasons she provided were deemed adequate by him. Pete wanted what he wanted, and anything less was not acceptable. Sensing that he was committed to his plan without exception, I made no attempt to pry him loose from his ego validation plan. Instead I supported him to stand up for his plan without hesitation. "I want sex with you three times a day and 21 times a week, and that is it!" Once Sally heard Pete repeat this mantra several times, she finally got the message that this was not a discussion or an option, and she replied simply, "I hear you." He said, "So will you do it?" Sally responded, "I hear what you want, and the answer is no." When Pete heard this, he attempted to go back to the debate, but she again stated only, "I hear you." Shortly after the argument cycle ended, they went their separate ways. Pete began to look for someone else with whom to pursue his plan, preferably a woman who needed this for her own validation.

Men never failed to notice Carnie who, at 35, had a voluptuous body, long blond hair, and drop-dead good looks. She devoted a lot of time and energy to her appearance, and dressed to emphasize her physical attractiveness which she felt was her main, and possibly her only, attribute. She knew she made quite an impression at nightclubs and would relish recounting the number of men who hit on her. She regarded this as her turf and would go there whenever she needed an ego boost. Her problem, like those of others in this plan, was that once a man was ensnared, he lost appeal, and she needed someone who wasn't impressed with her to fall under her spell.

The Rules of the *Status and Conquest* Dating Plan

- Only involve yourself with others who can enhance your ego in some way
- Pick partners who can assist you in proving something
- Regard the other as an object, not a person
- Think me, me, me

Who to Play With

- Good looking women/successful men
- People who buy into your ego trip

Upside of this Dating Plan

- Get to look good in the mirror
- Exciting while it lasts

Downside of this Dating Plan

- Roller coaster ride of highs and lows
- Disillusionment when bubble bursts

The Dynamics of the *Status and Conquest* Dating Plan

This is the plan for every emotionally little boy and girl who doesn't like being little. Its purpose is to use dating as a way to make you feel bigger and more important. It is likely that this plan will appeal to those who, at times, have felt inferior and suffered enormous pain and shame in regard to that perception. Dating, an activity that offers constant opportunities to be voted on, then becomes the means by which you can create a mental image of yourself as beautiful, successful, a sexual giant, desirable. If it works, you will get plenty of the applause you crave.

CHAPTER 8

THE *HIGH DRAMA* DATING PLAN

Many of us, bored with our lives, look for stimulation wherever we can find it. Relationships are a great way to provide us with a lot of excitement and drama.

Relationships offer us endless opportunities to pursue impossible situations, try to change others, see ourselves as victims, encounter hurt feelings, and fantasize romantic attachments out of thin air.

Some of the drama is created by our enormous expectations about what dating is supposed to do for us. It's supposed to fulfill our ultimate needs and dreams. In the movie *Beautiful Girls*, the character played by actor Randy Quaid states his desire to find a beautiful woman so he will no longer have to live a depressing, mundane life.

While many people complain about their dramatic relationship battles, it needs to be mentioned that these dramas can also be addictive. Once you get used to them, you may find yourself craving them, especially when things are calm. Missing the manufactured excitement of the dramatic, you'll want to do something to stir things up.

In order to practice the *High Drama* Dating Plan, it is best you forget everything you've learned so far in this book in order to act surprised and be totally shocked by whatever occurs in your dating relationships. Be blind to what you see right before your eyes, be deaf to what you hear, and be oblivious to all the red flags warning you to side-step a relationship you are willingly prepared to march right into. Take leaps before looking. Go against your better judgment. Seek out those exciting one-night stands.

Make unavailable people available, turn losers into winners in your mind, see the obnoxious as sweet, the passive as assertive, and by all means take on the job of saving addicts and alcoholics and gamblers and turning them into good citizens. All of these relationship choices will definitely bring a sense of intensity and high drama into your life that will rival the best soap opera on TV.

There are a number of potential partners for you out there if you decide to follow the *High Drama* Dating Plan. They all have the capacity to turn your relationship with them into one long, emotional scene. Picking someone who is a puffed up little boy or an inflamed little girl is a sure-fire guarantee that sparks will fly, especially if you do not agree with their views of the world. Someone who is highly defensive is also good, as is someone who will tend to personalize every comment you make and see it as an attack or an indication of pending abandonment. A good personalizer will take the most innocuous event and make a mountain out of it. Show up five minutes late and it will be interpreted as an insult, proving your lack of respect. Say that you'd like to spend an evening alone to catch up on some personal business, and it will be viewed as a threat to that person's security, if not proof of your attempt to end the relationship in a sneaky way. Deep hurt will follow that you'll be accused of causing. As you try to defend yourself, you'll find yourself in quicksand, going deeper into the drama of it all.

Jill had Dick constantly trying to prove his love, but every discussion became a circular blood bath.

Jill: You don't really want me.

Dick: Yes, I do.

Jill   Then how come you want to spend the evening with the guys instead of me?

Dick: It's only three hours.

Jill: That is three hours away from me. I knew you didn't love me.

Likewise Derek and Jin who made an art form out of creating drama in their relationship. There were absolutely no innocent events in their lives. Everything was turned into a drama, even events that most people wouldn't blink twice at.

Jin: How come you were late again?

Derek: It's only fifteen minutes.

Jin: You promised that you'd never be late.

Derek: Not if I'm delayed at work.

Jin: I called your work and you weren't there.

Derek: I was in the bathroom.

Jin: Did anyone see you there?

Derek: It's a bathroom for one.

Jin: I can tell when you're lying.

Derek: Why would I lie about being in the bathroom?

Soon, voices are raised, comments become more hostile, he feels pressured, she feels abandoned, and the drama is on again in all its glory.

Be aware that if you are a devotee of the *High Drama* Dating Plan, you're not going to get much else done in life. Your relationship will occupy most of your waking hours.

Even when you are away from your partner, you'll be ruminating over what happened during your last fight. You will feel exhausted on a regular basis, but not to worry, *High Drama* daters usually have a lot of endurance. They complain about all the chaos, but they don't stop it from happening.

You need to be careful who you pick to play with. If you've picked somebody who regards conflict as distasteful, you'll end up feeling frustrated. Getting a conflict avoider to play with you is like tossing a ball to a dog that just lets it lie there. What fun is that?

You'll end up missing the high drama so much you'll find yourself easily seduced back into it with someone else.

The *High Drama* Dating Plan offers several benefits. There's never a dull moment.

The boredom that occurs in committed relationships is unknown. Since the stimulation is high and breakups are a matter of course, sex can be great for a while. This is especially true when you start breaking up and then get back together again. But at a certain point you'll start to experience burnout. The sex thrill will drop to nothing and you'll start to scan the horizon for another partner to pep things up.

The Hollywood components are also enjoyable and addictive. Every day you get to play out an exciting, romantic movie in which you are the heavily put upon, but brave hero or heroine. Even more drama is generated by sharing the relationship with friends who often enjoy your re-enactment and are willing to live the plot complications vicariously, at least until they tire of it.

Cory was a 30-year-old woman who loved stimulation in any form, whether it was drugs, alcohol, or foreign men. She needed instant gratification and would jump impulsively into relationships that gave her an instant high, even though many of those were followed by a crash and burn. While she often said she wanted a stable, committed life some day, emotional drama was her drug of choice.

Following one sexual episode with a married man, she admitted feeling remorse about indulging in this relationship, even though she had found it intoxicating and unbelievably romantic. After telling him she wouldn't have sex with him, he picked her up bodily and carried her to bed. Of course, she melted. Now she was beating herself up over it. Why had she allowed herself to be swept into making love? She declared that she wanted to stop all the drama, but felt powerless to do so. In fact, she never had any intention of avoiding sex with this man. Her reluctance game was all part of the drama. When this was dramatized for her, complete with such protestations as, "Oh, God, I can't do this! It isn't right. I must go. Help me be strong!" she laughed. Soon she admitted what her true intentions had been that night, and that she had used drama because she didn't want to deal with him honestly. Eventually the more she owned her *High Drama* Dating Plan, the more relaxed and at peace with herself she became. Ultimately she confessed. "I'll tell you why I don't like real relationships," she said. "They're boring."

Rules of the *High Drama* Dating Plan
- Believe that the content that is discussed is real
- Break up often and then get back together
- Be deaf, dumb, and blind to what you are doing, and ignore red flags

- Expect your lovers to fill the giant hole that exists inside you

Who to Play With

- Match yourself up with an accusing, jealous, insecure, needy, or defensive partner
- Pick those who love chaos and stimulation, and have endurance
- Find someone you believe has the answer to your life and is holding out on you.

Upside of this Dating Plan

- Never a dull moment
- High drama gives you plenty of excuses to split

Downside of this Dating Plan

- It will take up your whole life
- Exhaustion will be normal
- There will be never-ending battles and arguments

The Dynamics of the *High Drama* Dating Plan

The major emphasis of this plan is distraction. The more drama, the more distraction is achieved. You may wonder why anyone would need so much distraction.

The *High Drama* dater believes that there are worse consequences than periodic noise and smoke. In their family of origin, they may have learned that if something uncomfortable emerges, such as infidelity, addiction, depression, emptiness, resentment, fear, or money problems, a lot of commotion will cover it up so the deeper issue is temporarily removed as a threat, and after several rounds of accusations, no one even remembers what it was. From their early years they fought against accepting life as being a cycle of interest and disinterest. Instead they would create this overwhelming dramatic interest to cover up a deeper sense of disinterest.

CHAPTER 9

👍 THE *I'M AVAILABLE TO THE* 👍 *UNAVAILABLE* DATING PLAN

The primary focus of this plan is to choose partners who are considered unavailable because they are married, geographically distant, emotionally crippled, or are off-limits – such as your teacher, priest, or therapist.

As with many of the other dating plans, the motive behind the *I'm Available to the Unavailable* Dating Plan is the desire for safety – safety from risk, from getting hurt, from being exposed. The beauty of this plan is that you get to avoid the risks while still experiencing an active dating life. Not only can you fall in love all you want, but your ego will get a boost because it will look like you are open to intimacy. You will tell yourself that the reason nothing permanent is happening is because the person you're seeing has a big availability problem. From time to time you may even hear yourself pleading with your unavailable partner to be more available so that you can have your dream relationship. But down deep you know that's never going to happen because that calls for a completely different dating plan.

Selecting geographically undesirable lovers is another way to manifest the *I'm Available to the Unavailable* Dating Plan. There's no worry that your partner will crowd you or make too many demands. You are free to long for more, knowing the safety of the distance makes that unlikely. It's a great excuse. "I'd really like to see more of you. Isn't it a shame we live so far apart?"

Typically those who select the *I'm Available to the Unavailable* Dating Plan will declare, "If he/she changed his/her mind/circumstances and became available, I would be there in a second." The implication, of course, is that you are up for an intimate relationship, but the other party isn't. The man I mentioned in the Comfort Zone chapter who presented two messages of interest and disinterest, was able to declare his interest in a relationship with one woman who expressed to no surprise…disinterest.

What's not acknowledged here is the fact that Mr. or Ms. Unavailable was selected precisely because he or she is not available for a committed relationship. The partner choice is no accident. If the other person were to suddenly become available, the dating plan would no longer work. You can't feel safe if you get involved with a married man, someone you can count on to have that permanent boundary, and then they leave their spouse and show up like a stray puppy on your doorstep, ready to be taken in.

In addition to the selection of an unavailable partner, it is important to pretend that the obvious limit doesn't exist. Susan, a 44-year-old single mother with two older boys, was one of these. She was in love with her former therapist whom she described as the love of her life. She would talk about the incredible feelings she had for him, the connection she experienced, and the certainty that this was mutual love. Yet they had never met outside the office, and he never said there would be more. The only relationship her therapist possibly wanted was a sexual fantasy and connection within the office boundaries. When questioned why she called a relationship with such obvious limits "love," she was offended. "You don't understand," she'd protest. "You probably have never felt a love such as this." When the therapist decided to cut off the relationship, telling her it wouldn't work, she was devastated. If only he'd have given them a chance instead of cutting it off, things would have turned out fine.

As is common with this dating plan, Susan carried on this relationship in her head long after the therapist-patient connection had been terminated, yet from the way she spoke of it, you would think the relationship ended yesterday. Her denial of his unavailability continued to feed her fantasy. Eventually she admitted that she was caught up in wishing he was different, just as she had done in a previous relationship with a married man. Safe relationships like this afforded her the opportunity of opening up her love feelings to the fullest, due to the safety of the fixed boundaries.

This is beautifully depicted by Edwin Friedman's fable, *The Magic Ring* in his book *Friedman's Fables,* in which a woman, who had been badly hurt by her ex-husband, wears a magic ring that allows her to pick only unavailable men, thereby removing the possibility of ever being hurt again. She could feel free to love with no danger of being in a lasting relationship, with no worry nor wonder where things might go. The wondering about where the relationship will end is taken out of the equation.

It is my belief that the word "love" is meaningless unless it is backed by a behavior in which both partners risk exposing themselves emotionally to the other and being willing to go through conflicts and obstacles together. That was not going on with Susan and her former therapist. When asked what she knew about this so-called love of her life, all she could say was that he was gentle and sensitive. Nor could she provide any specific instances of depth in the relationship. Clearly she was not fully ready to move to a different dating plan, but needed to stay with her *I'm Available to the Unavailable* Dating Plan until she was prepared to go for more. Eventually she did reach the point of wanting to date men who would be available to love her.

What about the unavailable partner in this plan? There must certainly be something in it for him or her, as it is not an altruistic act. The unavailable partner might just want someone to have sex with, a different kind of companion, or to feed their own fantasy.

Susan's former therapist had a strong need for some kind of relationship beyond the therapeutic one. Perhaps he was enjoying her adoration of him. Whatever the reason, it was something that was missing in his life outside the office.

Among the benefits of the *I'm Available to the Unavailable* Dating Plan is that there is no danger you will be asked to back up your feelings with any real commitment. Susan was able to continue her daily life with no interference. Her small, self-contained world remained the same. Only her fantasy became huge. Another benefit, similar to one in the *High Drama* Dating Plan, is the tremendous emotional drama created by this plan. When you are in the midst of this kind of relationship, there are no dull days. Every day is an exciting, romantic movie with you as the star. There is none of the boredom that occurs in committed relationships. The drama is intensified by sharing the relationship with friends, reliving the moment as they live it vicariously with you.

There are many consequences in this plan, especially for those unable or unwilling to acknowledge that they are using the *I'm Available to the Unavailable* Dating Plan. There are plenty of hurt feelings and a sense of being victimized by your lover. "How could he treat me this way?" or "Why won't he be more available?" And tremendous frustration.

"All I ever hoped for – Nirvana – is just around the corner. How can we be so close and yet so far apart? If only…"

Incidentally, the *I'm Available to the Unavailable* Dating Plan is a misnomer since everybody is available for something, even if it's to play "unavailable" to somebody else.

Susan's therapist was available to her by providing grist for her fantasy life and providing her with the kind of verbal connection she had never experienced with any other man. He just wasn't available to having an ongoing, everyday life relationship.

Rules of the *I'm Available to the Unavailable* Dating Plan

- Select only those who are clearly unavailable for a committed relationship
- Make sure they have some circumstance that limits their involvement with you
- Pretend that the limit doesn't exist

Who to Play With

- Someone who finds it important to have a relationship with built-in limits
- Someone who wants to use you in a specific way, such as sex or companionship

Upside of this Dating Plan

- A lot of drama
- You can open up your heart totally and experience guaranteed safety

Downside of this Dating Plan

- If not conscious of the rules, you are likely to feel terrible hurt

- Enormous frustration, because you will believe you are so close, yet so far
- Exhaustion trying to overcome the limit and change it
- Spending a lot of time obsessing about the future

Dynamics of the *I'm Available to the Unavailable* Dating Plan

The bottom line here is how to live without getting hurt. If you sign up for *I'm Available to the Unavailable* Dating Plan, you may feel you have already experienced too much hurt in your life and don't want any more. The earlier hurt you experienced was deemed to be too traumatic. On the flip side, you crave involvement. You are not a loner and need meaningful contact with others. In effect, this plan allows you to bring both desires together in the form of intimacy with no hurt.

CHAPTER 10

 **THE *PARENT/CHILD* DATING PLAN**

Most of us like to believe that when we enter the dating world beyond high school, we are leaving our mommies and daddies behind and are ready to meet the love of our life. But often we take our favorite roles from our early family years right into our new relationships. I frequently see people in treatment who were the caretakers in their families of origin, doing the same things as adults by mothering or fathering their partners. I'll hear a woman say, for example, "I have three children at home, and my husband is one of them."

The *Parent/Child* Dating Plan wouldn't work if there weren't so many people just waiting to be mothered or fathered, enabling them to continue endlessly with the little girl/little boy acts they learned in childhood. Those who play the little boy/little girl roles in relationships usually deny it, but their behavior tells us something different.

Underneath the bravado, they simply like to be taken care of, so it's fortunate that there are plenty of match-ups to go around.

Central to the *Parent/Child* Dating Plan is the issue of being needed. Individuals who select this plan have a strong need to feel important by having their partners look up to them for help and instruction. If you haven't felt important in other aspects of your life, such as work and school, or you just love being top dog, this is the dating plan for you.

Relationships offer you many opportunities to assume this role because there are plenty of situations that require help, from money to intimacy.

Proper selection of one's partner for this dating plan is the key. If two "teachers" pick each other, who will the student be? If you're a parenting-teacher type, you need to select a partner who is dependent on you in one way or another. Any passive "little boy" or timid "little girl" will do, giving you ample opportunities to guide, instruct, correct, and nurture. You can enlighten them about how to live life the right way. No matter what is happening with your partner, in the *Parent/Child* Dating Plan it is necessary for you to assume control by teaching them something. Even without their asking, find ways to instruct and correct them in order to establish your parenting position.

Millie, 50, had become an expert in mother/son relationships. She'd pick men who were younger and struggling – financially, emotionally, or career-wise – and then she'd teach them and guide them under the guise of helping them grow. There was rarely a time when she was the focus. Like demanding, active children, they were center stage 99% of the time. Millie liked to talk about what advice she needed to give her partner that week in order to cure him of his latest irresponsible act or inept way of dealing with the world. If he ever came up with his own solutions or tried to grow up, Millie would let him know how ineffective his solutions were likely to be.

She would often complain that her current boyfriend wasn't satisfying her as a woman.

That should have been no surprise as she chose her dates expressly for their need to allow her to mother them. Furthermore, she had little sexual interest, and a different kind of man would make sexual demands on her. For her, the *Parent/Child* plan was ideal.

Since the *Parent/Child* Dating Plan depends upon one of you being the parent and the other being the child, it is hard to generate much passion and sexual energy. Also, given the hierarchical nature of the relationship, growing up is out of the question. If you are sloppy in your selection and pick someone who is in the process of growing up, the termination of the relationship will loom large. When the partner succeeds as an adult, the relationship will be over.

Rules of the *Parent/Child* Dating Plan
- Place being needed above all other desires
- Control all dating relationships by being in the top position

Who to Play With

- Someone who is very dependent
- Someone who isn't likely to have a mind of their own
- Someone who acts like a little girl or little boy

Upside of this Dating Plan

- You always get to feel important
- You avoid having your own limitations in the spotlight
- As long as they stay little boys/little girls, your partner will never leave you

Downside of this Dating Plan

- Little sexual relationship or passion
- Need to be careful that the little boy or girl doesn't grow up

Dynamics of the *Parent/Child* Dating Plan

This plan suits someone who has idealized the role he played in his family of origin. It allows one to recreate an important identity that helped that person survive his childhood. Without this early parenting role, such as being the caretaker in a home with an alcoholic mother, the child may have felt he/she was of no value. Since being a successful caretaker gave the child value, he/she recreates that role in adult relationships.

Another vital dynamic here is familiarity. The role they have chosen is second nature to them and they have no worries about being seen as inadequate. Departing from a role they know so well would leave them on shaky ground, and they've designed their lives specifically to avoid these feelings. Therefore they continue to do what is most known and predictable to them.

CHAPTER 11

THE *RESCUER/SAVIOR* DATING PLAN

This plan is more extreme than the *Parent/Child* Dating Plan, although it involves many of the same mothering and fathering dynamics. In this plan it is not enough of a challenge to simply coach, correct, or improve your date in some task or situation. This plan requires a much more crippled individual to pair up with, so your accomplishment is clearly noticed by one and all. "He was an alcoholic when I met him, and now look – he's been sober for 90 days." It should be noted that it is better if the partner doesn't change totally, or you will be out of a job. A sober person who stays sober and gets his act together doesn't give you anything to rescue and save any longer, so you will need to move on.

Selecting someone who merely acts like a little boy or girl is hardly adequate for the *Rescuer/Savior* Dating Plan. That would be a joke to any heavy-duty rescuer, and not come close to utilizing their extensive talents. What you want to hear are appreciative comments from the community such as, "Boy, is he a handful!" or "How do you do it?"

These remarks are most apt to be elicited when you've opted to take on a really tough case.

In addition, the more your mate is crippled, the more opportunities for you to come up with ways to rescue and change them. Proponents of the *Rescuer/Savior* Dating Plan tend to read a lot of books about their partner's disability or addiction in order to educate themselves on how to change their dysfunctional partner into the Perfect Mate. Any books that could guide you on how to date alcoholics, borderlines, or drug addicts would be extremely helpful.

An addict of any stripe is a perfect date selection for the *Rescuer/Savior* Dating Plan, with alcoholics, drug addicts, gamblers, and sex addicts leading the pack. You also want someone with a fairly extensive track record, not a person who took up drinking last month. Also, only select people who would basically be considered losers, yet display some potential to be more than they are at present. You can always say they just haven't been exposed to the right circumstances. This provides you with the hook that keeps you going in your quest to rehabilitate them; you know they are worth it. Otherwise you might get disinterested.

Anita was struggling with a boyfriend who was an alcoholic, pot smoker, womanizer, liar, burglar, and, on top of all that, unemployed. She had a full time job monitoring him constantly to keep track of all his sleazy, dysfunctional, acting-out behaviors. Whenever she caught him at one of his transgressions, she'd drown him in verbiage and drag him into therapy, only to have him slip and fail. After years of doing this, the man made his failure permanent when he drove himself into a tree, ending his life.

Unless your partner goes and dies on you, the *Rescuer/Savior* Dating Plan has great staying power. Sure enough, soon after her boyfriend's fatal accident, Anita began living with another full-blown alcoholic who became mean when intoxicated. She regularly bemoaned her plight, and daily delivered lectures and threats to him about how he should grow up. In selecting this man so quickly after the last one, she made it difficult for herself to deny the dating plan she had chosen. What was so unacceptable about a regular relationship that drove her to engage in such a difficult dating plan? She revealed that in her early years she'd been called a geek, and it had left her with feelings of shame. She felt she was unlovable, and believed no solid, responsible man would ever desire her.

With the crippled men she was choosing, at least she could feel needed and loved, as they were too crippled to leave her.

It is not difficult to find the benefits of Anita's plan. Both men provided her with an enormous challenge in trying to change them. While many might question how meaningful it was for her to take on the job, Anita was always clear about why these men were worth saving – they had potential, and she was convinced that she had the ability to bring it to fruition. Most of us want to have a goal in life.

Even though it took tremendous energy for Anita to pursue a goal like this, it gave real purpose to her life.

The *Rescuer/Savior* Dating Plan is definitely not for the meek or those who lack energy. Those who favor this plan are usually exhausted and frustrated by it, but they persist. If you are not prepared to devote all your time and energy to your mate, this dating plan is not for you. It will expose you as unfit.

Nor is the *Rescuer/Savior* Dating Plan for you if you have aspirations toward your own personal development. There will be no space in the relationship for such frivolousness. This plan requires concentration 24 hours a day, 7 days a week! But in spite of the bleak picture, there is entertainment value in this plan. You'll always have something interesting to talk about over lunch with friends or relatives who will find the twists and turns in your relationship fascinating, offer lots of advice, and marvel at your dedication, courage, and tenacity.

Rule of the *Rescuer/Savior* Dating Plan

- Select partners who are crippled, yet seem to have potential to be more
- Obsess on what it would be like to help them change
- Create a never-ending list of ways for them to improve

<u>Who to Play With</u>

- Addicts of any kind
- Those who are not working, but seem bright
- Those who are going through heavy, never-ending emotional turmoil

<u>Upside of this Dating Plan</u>

- You will experience ultimate challenges
- You will always have a focus for your thoughts and energies
- Plenty of food for conversation with friends and relatives
- You will always feel important or needed.

<u>Downside of this Dating Plan</u>

- Exhaustion and frustration
- No time for your own development

Dynamics of the *Rescuer/Savior* Dating Plan

People who love to rescue are individuals who have felt a lack of value and meaning in their early lives, and stumbled upon rescuing as a way to get validated. Without this activity, they fear they would be nothing and attract no one. They made a decision at an early age, when they felt extremely powerless, that they had to find a way to make a difference, and saving others seemed like a fitting career.

CHAPTER 12

THE *I GET AHEAD OF MYSELF* DATING PLAN

No matter which dating plan you choose, you need to be able to support what the plan asks for, such as being willing to be uncomfortable or scared, otherwise the plan won't work. The *I Get Ahead of Myself* Dating Plan is the one exception to this rule. In this plan you are always involving yourself in relationships that you are not ready for. You will always be getting ahead of yourself as you enter a relationship that is more than you can support.

I wish I had a dollar for every time one of my clients didn't respect their own pace and got overwhelmed. One, who came to realize she was using the *I Get Ahead of Myself* Dating Plan, admitted, "When I stopped rowing, the relationship stopped." This is a very telling statement because people who utilize this dating plan are usually the ones supplying all the energy and doing all the work to keep it going. It's a house of cards, and one huff or puff blows it apart.

There are three kinds of people most suitable candidates for this dating plan. First are those who know all the right relationship words, but are in fantasyland when it comes to seeing what's really going on. Second, those who are so passive they can be led into having a relationship based on the needs of others because they love to please. Keep leading and they'll follow. Third, those who have no patience, never liked delayed gratification, and are intent on racing through life to achieve their goals.

The best thing about the *I Get Ahead of Myself* Dating Plan is that by being blind to what's really going on, you have the illusion that you're in control. The relationship is formed out of your desires, wishes, hopes, and dreams rather than by what's actually happening. Typically, you carry on the relationship regardless of what the other does or says. In effect, you are the relationship. The other party is just an object you picked to play this with, regardless of how they play their role. That is why, when you stop rowing, there's nothing there and the relationship sinks.

Barbara met Sean after the end of a fairly painful relationship with another man. She thought Sean was good, dependable, and sweet, but didn't feel attracted to him, nor was she in love with him. Still, she got ahead of herself by trying to make the relationship more than it was, and ended up marrying him. It was a disaster. Marriage was beyond what either of them could handle. Instead of respecting what the relationship was meant to be, possibly no more than a warm friendship, they married and ended up divorced, not even on speaking terms with one another.

I've seen several marriages end as a result of the *I Get Ahead of Myself* Dating Plan.

Getting ahead is a common behavior couples make. It usually occurs when the man pursues the woman very strongly, she ignores all the obvious red flags and negative messages, until she finally says, "All right, let's do it." Either she was feeling vulnerable at that time or she told herself that if he cared that much, love could transcend all the things she found missing.

Daphne met a man she suspected was seeing someone else, and wondered if she should ask him about the other woman. Yet she had only seen him in a group situation twice when he asked her to join him and his friends again. In other words, there was no relationship! Two group dates were just that – group dates. He was not her boyfriend. She had tried to get ahead of herself and act in a way this very tenuous relationship did not call for.

In our get-there-yesterday culture, the idea of not being ready for something is considered a problem to be overcome as quickly as possible. Nobody gets accolades for announcing to the world, "I am not ready for a commitment." As a result, many singles feel bad when they realize that this is exactly where they are – not ready. It's heard as an excuse, almost an avoidance of one's duty, and met with such responses as, "When will you be ready?" or "Just do it."

Not being ready is an issue that can come up during any phase of the dating plan spectrum, from not being ready to date at all (the *Date Nobody* Dating Plan) to not being ready to move beyond casual dating (the *On the Clock, Seeker,* or *Comfort Zone* dater), to not being ready to venture forth into bigger commitments (the *Extended* or *Long-Term Committed Relationship* dater). The stumbling block is not being ready to be afraid.

If you want to play the *I'm Ahead of Myself* Dating Plan, you can't play with people who *are* ready or people who attend to their emotional limits. It is best to be with partners who are also not ready for whatever the next step is in your relationship, but ignore this truth. Then you can each take turns flying by one another. Both of you can be not ready to have sex, commit, live together, or get married to name just a few possibilities. It doesn't matter what each person's justification is for going forward beyond what they can support; only that they do. Maybe it felt so good, or he wanted more, or I was in love. All justifications are masks for the bigger issue, that you were not ready to truly be afraid in taking that next step, or that there was no next step to take.

Although Jolene said she'd had enough of dating superficial men and wanted to date men who were more mentally and emotionally substantial, she was not ready for it. She needed first to come to grips with her underlying sadness. This was an overwhelming obstacle for her. "I don't like to be sad," she said. "If I let myself be sad, it will never stop." Jolene did not understand that experiencing her sadness would also allow her to experience her depth of feelings, something a deep relationship calls for. If she was unwilling to do so, she would have to continue to be satisfied with superficial men.

Sex is an issue that comes up a lot for *I Get Ahead of Myself* daters. You are ready for sex in a relationship, whatever your dating plan, if you know and can handle all the consequences. You need to be able to look at yourself in the mirror the next morning and feel good about the sex experience with no resentment or judgment about what you did.

You are ready for greater commitment when you are aware and accepting of the consequences and are willing to move ahead even though you are afraid. If you cannot meet these criteria, you are clearly getting ahead of yourself even thinking about sex.

People get ahead of themselves in dating because of desire. They think if they want something, such as a long-term committed relationship, they should try to promote their current relationship into an intimate LTCR. The fact that their partner can't even spell "intimate" doesn't stop them. They go forging ahead and usually find disaster.

Engaging in sex is one way that women, especially, try to promote their relationship into something more than it is. They get far ahead of themselves and fail to address the inevitable consequences. The sex doesn't create the intimacy they're looking for, they hate themselves in the morning, and they end up with hurt feelings.

Mandy decided she was ready for a long-term committed relationship. She was prepared to put a sign up in Times Square proclaiming how very ready she was for a relationship that would culminate in marriage. After all, she was 34 and it was time.

On weekends Mandy was seeing a man who flatly stated he was not interested in marriage, and yet she never disclosed to him that her goal was a long-term committed relationship resulting in marriage and children. She'd pick fights and feel depressed and rejected because she wanted more than he was ready to give her. Even so, she was unable to declare a boundary and let her lover know her real goal, because regardless of her rhetoric, she couldn't support an LTCR even if one had appeared. It was all posturing.

People can glowingly appear enthusiastic about the wonders of a committed relationship, but while wishing, hoping, and dreaming are one thing, the reality is quite something else. Daters who force themselves into attaining the dream often end up helplessly watching it collapse in a heap. Not being ready is not the problem it's made out to be. It is just where you are at a particular moment. When you honor your limitation, you will be respecting your integrity and move through dating at your own pace and time.

Dishonor and you will always be ahead of yourself, and you will find yourself stuck in this dating plan.

Many who practice the *I Get Ahead of Myself* Dating Plan have a lot of denial going on about it. They choose not to be conscious about what dating plan they have adopted, and rush ahead anyway. They tend to distrust what their gut is telling them about the relationship. They prefer to let their rationalizing brain talk them out of their instincts.

"Yes, I feel uneasy with her, but it's my problem. I just need to trust more." Or, "What he told me didn't make any sense. Maybe I heard it wrong." As long as you ignore the warning signs and dishonor and disrespect your own emotional limitations, you'll get ahead of yourself and soon get smacked upside the head wondering how it happened.

Pat's profile had been on the Internet for just two months, and she was already feeling overwhelmed with stomach pains. Men were coming at her from all sides, several of them pressuring her for an exclusive relationship. She was getting lost trying to keep up with their pace, and taking care of their agendas. She expressed great relief when I mentioned that their pace was not her responsibility, and she needed to move at her own speed.

Linda had been separated for over a year and was dating several men. She described them all as lacking quality, not serious, unable to commit, and not to be trusted. "How do I meet quality men?" she kept asking. The answer was obvious, she was still emotionally tied to her ex-husband and was sleeping with him, even though he was by now living with another woman. She could not meet quality men because she was not ready for a quality man, not ready to put both her feet into a committed relationship. Her desire was way ahead of where she was.

Rules of the *I Get Ahead of Myself* Dating Plan

- Pick partners based on your desire
- Ignore all obvious internal objections and red flags
- Rely on hoping and wishing and dreaming
- Go further into the relationship than you are able to emotionally support
- Ignore your problems and limitation

Who to Play With

- Someone who talks a good relationship game, but is just talk
- Someone who is as unready as you are
- Those who aren't honest with themselves and deny their unreadiness
- Moldable people
- Grandiose people

Upside of this Dating Plan

- Feel some control since you are the relationship
- Pride yourself that you took a leap after friends said you were too picky

Downside of this Dating Plan

- Emotional unhappiness

- The pressing need to race ahead of your war with boredom
- Too much time spent fantasizing
- Freaking yourself out by constantly going beyond your capacity
- Never getting to feel relaxed

Dynamics of the *I Get Ahead of Myself* Dating Plan

This is a plan for those who do not trust themselves and are not secure enough to recognize what they are or aren't ready for. They are also influenced heavily by a sense of scarcity, as if they must race against time to get the few suitable mortals that exist on earth. They end up anxious about fulfilling their desires and leave no time or space for their own limitations. A slow pace, patience, and being afraid are considered the ultimate enemies, to be avoided at all costs. The hope is that by running fast they can stay ahead of these demons.

CHAPTER 13

THE *IT'S TIME I GOT MARRIED* DATING PLAN

A long-term committed relationship culminating in marriage is the dating plan desired by most women and many men. However, it's a different thing when being married becomes more important than who you are marrying.

When you reach a certain age, usually around 35, if you're not married, people start looking at you a little funny and making comments like, "Maybe you're being too picky."

They may even accuse you of being self-centered as the reason you are not married. A 45-year-old male who has never been married is also up for scrutiny. "Is he gay?" At the least, it's a red flag. "Maybe he's a mama's boy."

Because followers of the *It's Time I Got Married* Dating Plan make marriage decisions based on external rather than internal reasons, there is a much greater inclination to rationalize away any objections, ignore certain questions, and deny particular needs

Let's say you're a woman who has adopted the *It's Time I Got Married* Dating Plan.

You meet a new man. He may not be everything you ever wanted, but he is decent – and he is there. You decide you would rather be married to somebody who is okay than wait any longer and risk ending up with someone less desirable, or worse – nobody.

Your partner may go along with the marriage plan, not so much because he is in love with marriage, but because it meets his own need for a constant companion, security, or sex. For him, as with you, it is more to get out of the dating circle than it is because he's interested in being married to you.

In spite of the lack of total authenticity in this plan, it will provide many people with the external pictures that have long existed in their head – a common household, being part of a committed couple, a family. It's a picture with a lot of appeal, and it can also provide you with the lifestyle, stability, and companionship you want and enjoy.

Millie met Rob when she was thirty. She had become tired of going through the dating routine of seeing someone for a while, then breaking up. Rob let her know from the outset that he was interested in getting married, and she saw that as a way out of the dreary dating pattern she had been experiencing. She figured she'd be content at last if she could create a stable married life. Even though she had some questions about Rob's suitability, especially when it came to passion and Rob's ability to communicate, she pushed these thoughts aside so she could pursue her *It's Time I Got Married* Dating Plan.

Millie went ahead and married Rob and things went fairly well for about two years until her unmet emotional needs began to manifest themselves. She realized she was bored silly. From then on, the relationship began to run downhill. Irritation and tension slowly replaced whatever good feelings and stability they had.

Suitable partners for the *It's Time I Got Married* Dating Plan are those who meet some of your standards, but not all of them. Ultimately there are not enough key qualities to allow the passion or interest to last for very long. Many times the presence of children prolongs the relationship and hides the fact that the couple connection died years before.

The major problem with the *It's Time I Got Married* Dating Plan is that the plan is an attempt to build your dream pictures from the top down rather than from the bottom up.

In almost every instance this will ultimately collapse, just as a house would if you started with the roof and added the foundation last. Signs of the collapse may begin with a screaming in your head: "I can't stand this shallow existence," or "I'm so bored that every man/woman I pass on the street is starting to look good." Either you will quell these voices or have an emotional eruption.

Rules of the *It's Time I Got Married* Dating Plan

- Fall in love with the concept of marriage
- Panic because time is passing, partners are scarce, and you must get a spouse
- Jump into marriage regardless of who, what, where, or why
- Put a high value on making your marriage visions come true

Who to Play With

- Anyone who agrees to go along with your goal
- Someone who doesn't ask questions about your motives and reasons
- Someone who wants to use you as much as you want to use them

Upside of this Dating Plan

- The relief of getting off the dating merry-go-round
- You get to realize your marriage pictures
- Achieving a life-style you like

Downside of this Dating Plan

- It's not enough
- Parts of you will scream for more
- You'll be driven to seek negative ways to feed your emptiness. Overeating, affairs, drinking, spending

- Sooner or later you'll want to jump ship

Dynamics of the *It's Time I Got Married* Dating Plan

Individuals who are attracted to the *It's Time I Got Married* Dating Plan are susceptible to the cultural conditioning that dictates they should be married and have families. Their marriage, their job, their lifestyle is their identity. They have never fully developed their own sense of who they are, and without these presentable images, they would feel lost.

Failure to follow this conditioning risks negative comments from the community, which in turn may lead to a generalized melancholia. The latter will result whenever you feel that you cannot stand being without others' approval. The lack of marriage approval weighs heavily on many people. The names for people who don't marry are rarely pretty.

While it would be nice if everyone could stand up for his own destiny and not passively succumb to the path of others, those who are not blessed with strong self-esteem will find such an individualistic stance a hard way to go. Following the *It's Time I Got Married* Dating Plan seems the lesser of two evils.

CHAPTER 14

THE *I NEED A FATHER/MOTHER FOR* MY *CHILDREN* DATING PLAN

When you think "dating," you probably visualize two people going through the normal mating dance, each one putting up with the usual problems in order to find a good match.

But in many cases there's a hidden agenda. One or even both daters may be on the lookout for a father or mother for their children. Behind the rhetoric of finding the love of one's life are questions such as, "Will this person be a good father/mother for my child? Can he/she provide the material things/ nurturing they will need growing up?"

This plan is about priorities. Are your own needs the most important, or those of your children? After all, you brought them into the world so it's your responsibility to see that they have every possible chance to make it physically, socially, emotionally, educationally, and financially. If you cannot manage that alone, your primary concern must then be to do whatever it takes to insure that your children are well taken care of.

Your own sexual, romantic, recreational, and social needs may also be important, but they will out of necessity take second place. Many *I Need a Father/Mother for My Children* daters put personal desires on hold until their parenting responsibilities are met, and the children are cared for and happy.

Carole, a 38-year-old divorced mother of a 14-year-old boy, whose father was barely present in his life, began dating a string of men who didn't seem to hold a candle to her. She was beautiful, bright, educated, and had a charming personality. In contrast, the men she picked seemed boyish and limited, not men who could challenge her mentally, emotionally, and spiritually. At first I was very puzzled at the men she was selecting, until we both realized she was doing this for what she saw as her son's welfare, not hers. Her current boyfriend was able to provide her son with material advantages. Her previous boyfriend had been warm and fatherly. She hadn't admitted this to herself before, and she seemed relieved to consciously acknowledge it at last.

Ironically, when Carole decided to break up with the more affluent man, he offered to buy a house for her and her son. The offer was so outrageous that it wasn't hard for her to turn it down. It helped her to further realize that she was not selecting this man for herself, she was choosing him for her son. Now clear on her motive, she asked her boy if he wanted her to select men for his sake. He said, "Mom, I am only going to be around for a few more years.

Please do what's best for you." She sheepishly admitted that her child seemed to be more mature, and that she would no longer leave her own wants and needs out of the mix.

When choosing partners for the *I Need a Father/Mother for My Children* Dating Plan, qualities like good looking, sexy, funny, intelligent, and sharp will play second fiddle to such characteristics as solid, dependable, secure, and economically solvent. As a result, you my end up feeling emotionally empty and start longing for a more intimate, passionate connection. That's the danger. Those significant factors are often unmet with this dating plan, forcing you to remind yourself constantly what your dating plan is and why you chose it. If your children are older, as Carole's son was, you can talk your dating plan over with them, but if they are young, that won't be possible. You need to make the decision on your own and then abide by the rules of the plan.

Rules of the *I Need a Father/Mother for My Children* Plan
- Put your own personal needs aside
- Make your children the number one priority

Who to Play With
- Partners who are best for children
- Solid, nurturing, dependable people
- Individuals who deny their own personal needs
- Partners with good parenting skills

Upside of this Dating Plan

- Pride yourself on being a devoted parent
- Children will probably be pleased
- There is a sense of security
- You can't be accused of being selfish

Downside of this Dating Plan

- Constant feelings of frustration and boredom
- Deep emptiness and discontent
- You will find yourself wanting more

Dynamics of the *I Need a Father/Mother for My Children* Dating Plan

The last thing in the world that someone who selects this plan wants is to think of himself as selfish and irresponsible. The man or woman who adopts it learned early on that you must take care of others first, especially your children, before you attend to your own needs. For some it is a reaction to a neglected childhood with parents who did not properly care for them. These people have made a commitment to themselves that their children will never experience that kind of pain. The attitude is common with people in struggling marriages who will say, "I'm not happy, but I'll stick it out for the children."

CHAPTER 15

THE *WE'RE WORLDS APART*
DATING PLAN

While it might be nice to meet someone who is a perfect match for us in every respect– age, economics, religion, race, education, intelligence, children, and looks – this is rarely the case. If we enter the dating world at an older age, we are more likely to run into mismatches, polar opposites, and people with baggage. We also bring along plenty baggage of our own, more than we had when we were 21. People who meet in their thirties or older frequently come with a smorgasbord of potential differences: children vs. no children, debt vs. no debt, older vs. younger, minimal work schedule vs. heavy, ex-wives vs. ex-husbands, and foreign vs. native. No dating service, however well devised to pair like with like, can cover the wide range of differences that may exist between two people.

Bob, 58, fell in love with a woman whose baggage included three kids, the youngest of whom was only seven. Bob had a child from a previous marriage, but that child was 29 and long since out of the home. Bob's dilemma was whether to accept the package deal or walk away. He ultimately decided on acceptance, but many men would not.

While temporarily living in Sweden, Reed fell in love with a woman, married her, and brought her back to the United States. He was initially pleased with his beautiful, blond bride, but problems began to crop up as soon as they returned to the United States. She could not find work, and did not adjust easily to her new country. Other conflicts developed, as well. His impatience and emotional volatility made for constant chaos.

After many quarrels, she flew back to Sweden, but returned the following week when they patched things up. You can imagine where the relationship went from there.

Celine, 38, Caucasian, had a pattern of selecting men of different races or nationalities – an African-American, an Arab, and one man who was Japanese. She got upset when her family was not as accepting of her mates as she thought they should be.

Don, 40, got involved with a 62-year-old woman. While he liked her, and they had several interests in common, he was struggling with the fact that she was the same age as his mother. He also had to deal with the strongly negative opinions of his father regarding the relationship.

If you choose the *We're Worlds Apart* Dating Plan, it is best to address the differences immediately. Agree to be accountable for selecting each other and committed to the idea that this is what you really want, whatever the consequences. Be well aware of your choice, understand what the downside might be, and be ready to "own" your partner as your choice no matter what anybody says.

Since you are knowingly taking on a relationship that has obvious difficulties, you cannot afford to be shocked and surprised when the consequences start rolling in. If you are Middle Eastern and you are going to marry into a middle class Jewish family, don't act shocked when some members of that family or yours, express their displeasure, whether behind your back or to your face. Don shouldn't have been surprised over his father's displeasure that Don's girlfriend was 22 years his senior. His choice was to deal with it or move on to a different dating plan.

Being with someone who offers you a glimpse into a different world can be very exciting. Exposure to new cultures, perspectives, and diversity can expand your horizons, stretch your comfort zone, and add considerable richness to your life. However, if you passively slip into a *We're Worlds Apart* Dating Plan without thinking it through, this kind of dating plan can be pure hell. There will be conflicts and arguments, and you are likely to be the target of all kinds of negative projections. This can drain and frustrate the best of us. I know one racially and economically mixed couple with different religions whose differences ended the marriage before they'd even

173

reached their first anniversary. That was the result of not acknowledging their differences early on in the relationship, not discussing whether or not there was any possibility that one of them would accept religious conversion, nor determining creative ways to accept their mutual differences.

Rules of the *We're Worlds Apart* Dating Plan

- Fall for someone of a different age, race, religion, educational or IQ level
- Disregard that they are a package deal with all of their differences
- Spend no time addressing how the two of you plan to deal with these issues
- Tell yourself that your love will overcome all consequences
- Do not listen to feedback from friends or relatives
- Allow yourself to be entranced by the fantasy of going down a unique path

Who to Play With

- Someone who is very different from you
- Someone who wants to make a statement to the world
- Someone who is exceptionally flexible on issues
- Someone who doesn't care about the opinions of others

Upside of this Dating Plan

- It can add excitement and richness to the relationship
- Provides continual heated discussions to reduce boredom
- If successful, you will feel like you are fulfilling a movie fantasy

Downside of this Dating Plan

- Endless conflict and persuading
- Can be very draining
- Issue will often involve an entire family network, so you will need a hall to discuss each decision

Dynamics of the *We're Worlds Apart* Dating Plan

People who are attracted to this dating plan are often those who want to break away from their own conditioning and take a separate path. They think dating somebody who is worlds apart will help them establish their own identity and make a statement to the world. In a way, they want to use the relationship as a testimonial to how far they have come in leaving their roots. The trouble is, they often underestimate the obstacles they may have to face, and hold on to some grandiose view of themselves as above all that.

They fail to appreciate the process in which differences need to be recognized, integrated, and fully accepted into one's life.

CHAPTER 16

THE *EXTENDED RELATIONSHIP*
DATING PLAN

There are many single people who don't like to date around, but instead prefer the company of just one person. At the same time, they avoid being in any relationship with both feet, as they are not interested in marriage or being 100% committed. Extended relationships can last six months, three years, even longer, but eventually the relationship will end, often when one of the partners starts pressuring the other to move into a more permanent phase, such as marriage. This leads to arguments, and when it becomes obvious to both partners that things will not be going beyond this point, there's a split.

The *Extended Relationship* Dating Plan is a tricky dance because you seem to be deeply involved in the relationship and may even be living together. Yet you always need to make sure that you don't commit to it fully. It's a delicate balance. Sometimes what works is to state right up front that you are not interested in marriage, but this can backfire and you may lose your partner right then and there. It may be better if you can come up with some sort of justification for your independent stance, something that sounds legitimate. "I was so hurt in my former marriage that I'm gun shy," is often effective. From time to time your justification, whatever it is, will inevitably have to stand up strongly to numerous repetitive questions.

Extended relationships can also lead to prolonged, repetitive discussions. Marti and Jack lived together comfortably at first, but after a time they got stuck over the issue of having children. Marti insisted that she would only agree to marriage if she was sure Jack was open to having children. He balked, questioned her parenting skills, and made it clear he thought she'd be such a terrible mother. They went back and forth about this topic endlessly. After a while he almost convinced her he was right. Then it started to become apparent that he didn't want children. He had tried to convince her the problem was hers in order to dissuade her from wanting them. During all their discussions and fights, it appeared that if they could just resolve the child issue, they could move ahead to the marriage.

You are free to engage in the *Extended Relationship* Dating Plan with anyone who is willing to join your hedging rhetoric. People who have their own reasons for not wanting to move beyond this dating plan into an LTCR dating plan will be very suitable partners.

Many times a good partner is someone who is too afraid to stand up for his own needs, and will go along with your needs out of fear of losing you.

The *Extended Relationship* Dating Plan has some definite benefits which include a familiar and constant companion, an on-going sexual relationship, and a relatively good relationship with limited risk. It provides good value for your dollar. It is also an excellent plan for those who want to avoid the hassle and discomfort of the dating scene.

As long as your partner doesn't complain too much, the *Extended Relationship* Dating Plan has few consequences, until your partner becomes stronger about his or her own needs, or begins to see this plan as a dead end. At that time it can become very draining and frustrating, and you may dread going home if you are living together, or making a phone call that could end in confrontation.

Rachel and Charles had been together on and off for five years. Neither one of them saw the other as someone they could totally commit to. Charles was reluctant because Rachel didn't want any more children, as she had two already. Rachel expressed doubts about whether Charles was the kind of man she could rely on, as he was unsophisticated and stingy with money. Yet they kept coming back to each other saying that there was no one else they felt as comfortable with.

Rather than respect the limits of their *Extended Relationship* Dating Plan and be direct about it, Rachel would typically start fights whenever they got too close emotionally, in order to push things back to a psychologically comfortable distance. For his part, Charles would hook into whatever it was she brought up, instead of seeing what the real purpose of these fights were – to keep this mutually agreed-upon distance.

When couples complain that their relationship isn't going anywhere, it's often because they don't want to fully admit to the dating plan they're using. Moving beyond that would put them into another dating plan, such as the LTCR Dating Plan. In the *Extended Relationship* Dating Plan, one foot out and one foot in is the name of the game.

Rules of the *Extended Relationship* Dating Plan

- Never put both feet into the relationship
- Make sure you don't have a full "yes" for your partner
- Hold something out
- Justify why the relationship can go no further

Who to Play With

- Someone who also is reluctant to put two feet in and risk all
- A partner who buys into your justification
- A person who rationalized that they don't want to push you

Upside of this Dating Plan

- You get to be with someone you are familiar with

- You always have a companion and sex partner
- You get a good relationship ride with only moderate commitment
- The illusion of freedom

<u>Downside of this Dating Plan</u>

- After a time there will be dissatisfaction and tension
- Your partner will throw a lot of hurt your way in the end
- Many discussions about why we are not going further

Dynamics of the *Extended Relationship* Dating Plan

People who find themselves involved in this dating plan believe it is dangerous to put all their eggs in one basket. They may have gotten this message back when they were young. Perhaps they learned they couldn't fully depend upon their parents, that it was unsafe to do so, and they brought this uneasy expectation into adulthood. At the same time, they are definitely not loners. They have a strong need to be engaged in a relationship, so the *Date Nobody* or the *On the Clock* Dating Plans would have no appeal to them. In sharing the *Extended Relationship* plan with their partner, they've created a bargain that says, "Let's leave the back door open," hoping this will meet both their needs. So long as it does, the boat won't rock.

CHAPTER 17

THE *LONG-TERM COMMITTED* RELATIONSHIP *(LTCR)* DATING PLAN

This is the plan most daters, especially women, say they are aiming for. But it's one thing to say it and quite another to be able to support it emotionally.

There are two kinds of people who will make the *Long-Term Committed Relationship (LTCR)* Dating Plan their choice – the pseudo-committed dater who likes the idea of being in an LTCR, but is clueless about what it involves, and the sincerely committed dater who is into the LTCR heart and soul.

Pseudo-committed daters take on the image of commitment, but can't support the substance of this kind of relationship. They are largely unconscious about why they've picked this dating plan. Many express great interest in having someone commit to them, but have little awareness of what it means to commit to somebody else. They are, for the most part, posers, more into appearance than substance.

If an LTCR is just an image you want to put forth to the world, then you need to select someone who is willing to co-star in your movie about a committed couple. Many pseudo-committed types choose partners who are emotionally closed and distant, and consider vulnerability worse than the plague. When I ask pseudo-committed partners to tell me who their partner is deep inside, they cannot do it because that kind of intimacy isn't there, no matter how long they've been together or consider staying together. So while they think it sounds good for them to say they are in an LTCR, the real demands of such a relationship are more than they can deal with. They aren't willing to take the required risks and face the fears that such relationships demand. Some should probably consider another dating plan.

In *Surrendering to Marriage*, Iris Krasnow says that the real test for this kind of relationship is whether you can get through the boredom and tedium, not the vacations and romantic moments. An LTCR includes all of your humanity from security to insecurity, as well as all of your imperfections and inner struggles. If your date says that isn't his cup of tea, then this relationship will last only as long as you keep providing the acceptable pictures that he likes to see.

Ten Signs of *LTCR* Readiness

How do you know when you are ready for an LTCR? I have found at least ten readiness signs in the couples I've studied.

1. They walk instead of run
2. They screen their partners carefully
3. They stop, look, and listen
4. They choose partners on all four levels: mental, emotional, physical, and spiritual
5. They appreciate the importance of being a "we" not just two "I's"
6. They have patience
7. They are open to giving and receiving
8. They have moved beyond competing and comparing
9. They are able to hold on to and be themselves in the presence of the other
10. They are willing to be scared

Sincerely committed daters move slowly in their relationships, recognizing that a bond is created only by taking the necessary steps along the way. They are aware that it can't be rushed. They know that getting way ahead of themselves by impulsively jumping into an LTCR usually ends in disaster, so they prefer walking to running.

This direction is difficult because we live in a hurry-up culture that looks favorably on running. Walking doesn't have the same intensity and excitement, but it is the only way to give yourselves the time to truly know each other. Try to look at someone as you race by them, and tell me what you see. I would guess not much. Yet that is exactly what happens if you don't slow down the involvement and let yourself see, hear, and feel the other so you can let that whole person in.

In addition, walking puts the emphasis on observing, rather than on reacting. It lets you hear what the other person is really saying or not saying, and prevents you from accepting wishes and illusions as truths. Daters on the walking path recognize red flags as effective screening devices that will save them a lot of grief in the long run. They are willing to fully stand up for this plan, and expose those who are just posing as LTCRs. Those who go on this path also spend a good deal of time mutually sharing who they are, as well as asking the important questions. "What point are you at in your life?" "What kind of relationships are you used to?"

Committed daters are not interested in halfway measures. They only select dating partners they feel a "yes" for on all four levels – mental, physical, emotional, and spiritual. They see their relationship as a "we," are interested in mutual support and satisfaction, and are willing to be deeply touched by the other. A person who is interested in this direction fully realizes the importance of substance over presentable images. From that perspective, you will regard the person you are committing to as your reflection, not some accidental involvement. Additionally, they have a deep appreciation for being able to equally give and receive, and have moved beyond competing and comparing. Another essential characteristic of people who are ready for this plan is being able to support your feelings and thoughts in the presence of your partner. Failure to hold on to yourself will lead to resentment and the dilution of your love for each other.

Finally, committed daters are willing to be scared in the relationship – willing to stand up for themselves even when it's uncomfortable, express their own views and needs, confront when it's appropriate, and not sit on resentments. It's scary stuff, but it's what successful LTCRs call for.

Zora had been longing for a relationship for many years and had seen many men come and go. Now at age 35 she had just gotten engaged and was to be married within a year. Yet she felt insecure about the relationship and questioned her lover's caring for her. This was unconscious subterfuge. With this engagement she was facing more security than she had ever known. She was, indeed, scared – scared of the security and where she had never gone before, and she was being asked quite forthrightly by her fiancé's actions if she was willing to be really afraid of receiving this new security.

Kevin had little experience with a committed relationship, and now he was in one. He and his partner had just decided to be exclusive, share words of love, and begin to spend every night together. Suddenly all he could focus on was her abundance of male friends

As thoughts of it consumed him, he started to make little sarcastic comments to her. Like Zora, he had also gone where he hadn't been before and had stepped over the safe line in his life. He was extremely frightened of having a woman be there for him to this extent and had no idea how scared he was of being in an intimate relationship in contrast to longing for one.

Here are some questions you can ask yourself to help you determine whether or not you are involved in a successful LTCR:

- Do my partner and I both have the ability to soothe our anxieties?
- Can we allow a loving silence?
- Are we both comfortable with conflict and tension?
- Are we willing to be scared, sad, angry, apologetic?
- Are we both open to sharing vulnerable parts of ourselves?
- Do we own up to our limitations?
- Are we both open to discussing relationship issues when they come up?
- Can I imagine living the rest of my life with my partner without feeling I'm settling?

The *Long-Term Committed Relationship* Dating Plan makes the strongest demands, but it also provides the greatest benefits. A good LTCR can feed you in many ways and offers great fulfillment. It can give you the opportunity to grow and develop. It is a great teacher in all areas of life. However, don't expect all the benefits from an LTCR will simply drop into your lap from the beginning. It takes time and work.

Since this plan requires that you put the most in, there is great potential to be hurt if it ends. You will not want to take up this plan if staying safe is your goal. In LTCRs, hurt goes with the territory. An LTCR can also force you to come face to face with your shadow side, those parts of you that you deem unacceptable. Many consider this kind of exposure far too dangerous to risk. Yet it is nearly impossible to be in a truly intimate long-term relationship and manage to avoid being seen.

The Rules of the *Long-Term Committed Relationship* Dating Plan

- Go slow. Walk, don't run
- Be willing to be scared in your relationship
- Select only those you feel "yes" for on four levels
- Support a "we" relationship, not two "I's"

Who to Play With

- Someone who matches all of the above
- Someone who can be accountable and not personalize everything
- Someone who trusts themselves and can allow mutual dependence

Upside of this Dating Plan

- It can fulfill most of who you are

- You will grow emotionally and mentally

- You will feel nurtured and a part of a dynamic relationship

Downside of this Dating Plan

- Asks you to make a long journey and overcome many stumbling blocks

- Exposes your shadow side

Dynamics of the *Long-Term Committed Relationship* Dating Plan

This plan separates the men from the boys and the women from the girls. To choose this plan you need to be able to handle whatever comes up in the relationship without defending, blaming, or running away. It's for those of you who no longer are afraid of being afraid and are able to regard your fears as part of who you are and not your enemy.

You will also have learned to be accountable for your behaviors and feelings, and come to see that love is a behavior not a feeling. You are ready to be seen and see another as an equal partner, and claim the intimacy that goes with that commitment.

PART IV

THE STEPS

CHAPTER 18

THE STEPS TO AUTHENTIC DATING

I work with many single people in the midst of a variety of dating struggles. One common thread among them is that they want to leap from wherever they are on the dating path to their dating wish list. Well, dating is not about leaping, it has much more to do with taking the steps that your particular dating journey calls for. I want to illustrate these steps by going through one of the dating plans and showing what occurs when one moves from unconscious dating to conscious, from judgment to acceptance, from unaccountable to accountable, and from dishonoring to honoring the integrity of each plan. The plan I will focus on is the Drama Plan, which is very popular in our high-stimulation culture.

1. Recognize and accept your dating plan without judgment

Typically, single people who are advocates of this plan will either have no awareness that they crave drama or frequently tell me that this is true of their dating pattern, but they don't like it and it makes them very unhappy. In the first instance they will regard each drama dating experience as a surprise in which something just happens to them and they have no control over it. "I had no idea he was dating three other women." Those who express dislike for drama will make numerous gestures that they want to change this plan, but not really want to go through what that means.

This step addresses both of these claims. When someone shares with me a pattern of dramatic dating experiences, I flat out say to them that they are experts in creating the drama. How else could they explain such consistency? If they further object to this perception, I ask them for the unique skills they use in maintaining such a plan. When they fill a page with all their techniques, it becomes much harder for them to deny that they are drama masters. After all, the creation of constant drama does take great effort. If you have ever watched the Soaps, none of the men and women ever look at each other without a sense of distrust or suspicion.

Once there is an agreement that drama is clearly the plan of the moment, it is necessary to learn to accept it without judgment. There is no acceptance when phrases are expressed that include "I do drama, but I don't like it," "Drama makes me miserable," or "I don't accept the drama, but I do tolerate it." To accept a drama plan it is essential that there be no statements that indicate judgment, dislike, displeasure, or disappointment. Instead, it is necessary to state "I accept that I prefer drama dating over any other plan."

I agree with Debbie Ford who wrote *The Dark Side Of the Light Chasers*, that a person needs to keep saying this until there is absolutely no judgment or emotional reaction in order to truly accept it. Any avoiding gesture is considered an emotional reaction. When you can say this as merely a truth of your life with nothing to prove or defend, then you have fully acknowledged your acceptance of the drama plan.

2. Own Your Dating Plan

A common occurrence for daters who quickly profess their desire to change a plan is that they haven't been accountable for the plan in the first place. Many people know the presentable thing to say, especially about a plan such as drama. "I wish I could just have a stable, peaceful, easy relationship." While this may sound good to your family and friends, it means nothing if you haven't owned this plan. The rule is that you can't let go of what you haven't owned.

To get singles to own their drama plan, I ask them to express some version of the following quote as their clear, active choice, and not some passive event.

"I choose a drama plan because there is never a dull moment. It is constant excitement. In fact, every interaction, no matter how little, can become a source of high intensity. No longer do I have to worry about boredom, mediocre, or routine like so many other relationships struggle with. After each breakup I get to start new all over again. And I can create all this stimulation without any use of drugs or alcohol. Yes, there are times when the fighting is exhausting and overwhelming, but I'd accept that consequence any day over a lifetime of dull. An added bonus is the intense love making when I get you reunite for the moment."

When you can own any plan in this manner, the candid honesty can feel very freeing.

3. Embrace Your Plan 100%

In deepening your ownership of your dating plan, you need to embrace it 100% from head to toe with total passion. Anything less than this will constitute a hedge and create a split inside you. When this happens, a part of you will be choosing the plan and a part of you will be fighting against it. It doesn't matter if 80% is for it and 20% rejects it. You will still be split and won't experience the joy that is inherent in any plan.

I'm sure there are many of you who doubt that intense drama can be joyful, and initially the people I work with possess the same doubts. The only way to accomplish truly knowing this is to allow the following experience. I ask my drama plan person to live their plan totally for seven days with their partner. So instead of unconsciously slipping into the drama over some trivial event, feeling righteous rage, then feeling bad, apologizing for the hundredth time, and then repeating the cycle, I invite them to do drama on purpose and love every moment of it for a week.

Openly announce and tell your partner up front. "I am going to create drama and intensity like you have never seen it. I will use everything that occurs in our week as an opportunity to further the drama, and I am going to do my best to hook you into the plan. I know that usually you are on guard as to when I am going to create drama. This week you won't have to wonder because I am going to do it with everything in our life and enjoy every minute of it. In the end I will not be doing my usual apology dance which you never trust anyway. Instead I will be cheering my accomplishment."

When you can go through seven days of embracing your drama plan, an unexpected shift will occur within you. By giving yourself total permission to express and embrace your plan, you will be in control of your drama for the first time and no longer feel that your drama runs you.

4. Only Select Partners Who Fit Your Plan

If you were into tackle football, you wouldn't choose to play with people who were only comfortable with touch or flag football. You would pick someone who gets off on the aggression of a full contact sport. The same is true here with the drama plan. A partner who can't stand any intensity, conflict, or anger, and prefers a quiet, serene existence would certainly not be suitable. It is no fun to do the plan all by yourself. You need a playmate.

Now, especially in this plan you will find people who protest about playing the drama game, but despite this lament, they will easily hook into the chaos. This person is fine to play with, and their protests and complaints just add to the intensity.

I directly ask my drama plan participants if they have selected well. I will even offer them someone who might be a better player, or if they are posing as being tired of the plan, I will invite them to be with a quiet, no conflict person. Typically they go running back to their familiar drama partner.

5. Be Aware Of Red flags

As with any plan, there are warning signs which indicate there is going to be a problem in being effective with your plan. This is especially important because this plan calls for an enormous amount of energy and effort, and drama slackers cannot be tolerated. Some of the red flag indicators for weak qualifications are present if you hear any of the following expressions:

I don't like arguing or conflict.

I like to go slow in a relationship.

I have a high frustration tolerance, and I'm comfortable with delayed gratification.

I don't get very attached to people.

I am an excellent pleaser.

I have no need to defend anything.

If you hear or see any of these comments or anything similar to them, then you need to head for the door, or boredom is going to be on your doorstep.

6. Honor the integrity of your plan

Every plan has its own integrity which speaks to the nature of that dating experience, and the drama plan is no exception. To be true to this plan as well as the others, it is necessary to respect what each plan is and what it is not. The drama plan is known for its up and down movement with quick swings. This is what accounts for the intensity and high emotional reactions. It is similar to a roller coaster. You don't see many people feeling calm as they ride on one of those.

Since there is a good deal of accusing, blaming, defending, threats, and lack of accountability, the noise level will be very high. All of this is fed by a constant rhetoric attesting to having the biggest hurt or being unequivocally right. Safety is out of the question here.

Any objections to this scenario indicates that you are not respecting the drama plan. Ask yourself the following questions to determine whether you are honoring this plan.

Are you enjoying the intensity?

Are you getting a charge from the emotional swings?

Are you appreciating the tension of never knowing if the relationship is alive or dead?

Are you loving the fights, never-ending arguments, and the getting back together?

If your answers are yes to all of these, congratulate yourself as being a professional, successful, and authentic drama plan player.

7. Have you out-lived your plan?

Each plan is not typically played for your entire life and only will fit you for a period of time. When things begin to change, it is then time to move on to another plan. The following questions will provide clues to you that your drama days may be over.

Are you no longer feeling the same excitement from the dramatic moments?

Are the swings, fights, and threats starting to feel old and repetitious?

Are you feeling like you could act out the plan without even showing up and know every line before it is even said?

Are you finding in response to your partner's provoking invitations, you are having trouble motivating yourself to join in?

Do you find yourself longing for a stable relationship that is not threatened on a daily basis?

Again, if the answers are yes, then it is probably time for you to retire from the drama plan because you no longer have what it takes.

By now, you possibly have noticed that all of the steps invite you to move toward the essence of each plan, in this case drama, when the normal tendency is to move away or try to get rid of that quality. To move against anything only makes that aspect of yourself more intense. Thus, I strongly support people to go with the river, unless some of you identify with being a salmon. In order for you to truly trust what I am saying, you will need to experience these steps yourself. Try it and see. If it doesn't work, you can always go back to attempting to get rid of whatever you deem unacceptable.

PART V

THE QUESTIONS

CHAPTER 19

FREQUENTLY ASKED QUESTIONS ABOUT PERSONAL DATING PLANS

Now that you've studied and possibly even tried one or more of these 15 Personal Dating Plans, you may have questions. Here are several that come up frequently when someone is attempting to apply this unique personal dating plan concept to their lives.

How do I know which of the 15 dating plans is right for me?

There is only one dating plan that is right for you at a given time. In order to grasp this, you will need to let go of your conditioned thinking with its emphasis on more or less, and shift to viewing dating as doing whatever fits you at a particular time. *Dating Nobody* is no better or worse than being in an intimate LTCR relationship. The right plan for you is the one that you can support emotionally and mentally, and the one that reflects your current truth.

What are the most important things to keep in mind when choosing a dating plan?

Your priorities. Go back to Chapter 2 and review question #3: *"What are your priorities?"* The answer to this question reveals the bottom line in many of your relationships because the dating plan you pick is always the one that's based on what your priorities are at a particular time in your life. Not only will your priorities dictate what somebody can expect from you in a relationship, but your partner's priorities will dictate what you can expect from him.

For example, if work is your number one priority you are most likely to want to *Date Nobody*, or have very limited relationships. However, if having a safe existence is your number one priority, you will most likely gravitate to a *Comfort Zone Plan*, while the importance of a passionate love commitment will be merely a thought, at best.

What does it mean to be responsible or accountable for my dating plan?

Being responsible or accountable means you consciously choose your dating plan, you don't just fall into it with no awareness. You pick, own, and support your dating plan 100%. You don't kid yourself or others about what you're up to. Your dating plan reflects where you are emotionally, mentally, physically, and spiritually. Your behavior needs to match what you say is your dating plan, and you need to be willing to accept the consequences of that dating plan, rather than be surprised by it.

In the 15 dating plan chapters, all these consequences are spelled out. However, many daters don't like to admit to themselves or others which dating plan they've chosen. One particular Comfort Zone dater was so vague that even the woman he was dating wasn't sure they were dating. He was reluctant to admit to her that he preferred being vague and evasive, so that she couldn't accuse him of letting her down in the future. The more anyone views their personal dating plan as unacceptable, the less likely they are to be accountable for their choice.

There is no way to practice conscious dating unless you take responsibility for your dating plans. If you are reactive rather than proactive, you will see yourself as a passive recipient of what happens. You will blame external causes and your partner for your dating displeasure. I call this living outside-in, which is in contrast to living inside-out, where you recognize that you are the cause of your dating experiences.

Outside-in daters commonly use the word "if." They indicate they'd be able to change their dating plan "if" the universe would first provide them with what they want. "Show me the woman or man I can have a committed relationship with, and then I will make the necessary internal changes and open myself up." This is a great formula for being an unconscious dater, but little else.

Switching from the "if" school to the "creator" school is vital for conscious dating.

You need to be accountable for your dating selections, plans, and behaviors. Making choices that are less than 100%, avoiding responsibility for your choices, will only leave you depressed, frustrated, and uncomfortable. If your heart is only involved 50% in a dating plan, you will be anxious or angry the other 50%. Yet you may be concerned that if you enter into something 100% you'll be stuck there for the rest of your life.

Paradoxically, the opposite is true. When you can own your dating plan choice 100%, you will have the greatest possibility of moving on to another dating plan.

How long should I commit to a single dating plan?

There are no "shoulds." You are only committed to a dating plan as long as it fits you and is reflective of what you are ready for. Don't get ahead of yourself and attempt to move on prematurely. Do it only when you have outgrown a particular dating plan. On the other hand, don't linger too long in dating plans you've outgrown. Learn to recognize when a plan has grown too small for you. Be honest, and don't underplay yourself by indulging in negative self-talk.

Do I tell my dates about my personal dating plan preferences?

Most daters worry that revealing themselves will lead to damaging results. They're afraid of getting hurt or hurting their partner. What they do instead is attempt to hide their real dating plans and leave it up to their dates to guess what's going on between the two of them.

If your date can't handle your honesty about who you are and what your dating boundaries are, then he or she is not going to be open to it or comfortable with it later on. By the end of the first five or six dates, if your date can't accept your directness, things will not likely improve from there. I recommend you be authentic, accountable, and conscious – and let the chips fall where they may. The only exception being when it is totally obvious that your date would have no clue as to what you are talking about.

A woman shared with me her uncertainty about whether to reveal something about herself to her date. She feared it would cause him to reject her. I said, "What if it did?

Sharing things can be a great screening device. You'll learn about the emotional and mental limitations of the person you are dating. If he rejects you, you'll know what his capacity is, and you will have saved yourself a lot of time. Remember, it's his limitation. It doesn't mean there's anything wrong with you. On the other hand, if he doesn't reject you, you may end up being in an involved relationship. If that's not what you want, be careful about which game you choose to play."

When you don't express who you are, you demean the other person. Focusing on protecting your image, such as being a good person or nice guy, leads you to ignore your real thoughts and feelings. When you hold back something about yourself, you are telling your date that he doesn't have the capacity to experience who you are and is somehow a small, limited, inadequate person.

What if my date doesn't agree with my dating plan?

Your dating plan is yours and is not subject to the opinion of others. If your date is uncomfortable because your dating plan interferes with his, it will result in a mismatch.

For example, if you want a brief fling and your date wants a long-term relationship, the two of you will have to face this and decide what's to be done. Each of you may end up disappointed that the other has a different dating plan that must either be accepted or rejected. Stifling the disappointment or trying to appease the other person does not work for long.

How do I handle criticism from others about my dating plan?

One of the main things this book advocates is not giving others the opportunity to vote on you. What you do is what you do, it is not up for a vote. If you remember this, people's criticism will have less power over you. If you choose to date a married man, you don't have to hand out ballots so others can vote on it. It is up to you to proceed with your personal dating plan and accept the natural consequences of your choice. If you can do that, your dating plan will work for you as long as you need it.

How do I avoid being rejected?

You can't. When you step into the dating world there will be rejection. Choosing to date is choosing to be rejected. For many, bailing out in advance seems preferable to risking possible rejection and discomfort down the line. You can limit rejection by not dating or exposing yourself only to those who will be the least likely to hurt you, or you can work night and day to make yourself so irresistible that no one will dare reject you.

But even then, somebody somewhere will reject you for trying too hard!

Motivational speaker and writer Anthony Robbins says that all of us are motivated by the avoidance of pain. Many single people have decided that being hurt by another is a pain to be avoided at all costs, and have declared they will not let themselves be hurt again. That could lead to a very lonely life, unless you decide that loneliness is more painful than rejection.

How can I reject someone without hurting them?

This is the flip side of the question above, and it's a common concern. Just as dating opens you up to being hurt and rejected, it also exposes you to disappointing others, unless you're willing to marry somebody you can't stand just to avoid hurting his feelings.

Many people hate the idea of disappointing someone else. What if he needs you? What if you feel an obligation to him? What if he gets angry? All of this is part of the dating territory, and your task is to honor the integrity of each dating situation. Give yourself permission to disappoint others and let their loss touch you without hedging your honesty.

To illustrate the extent that some people will go in order to avoid dealing with this experience, a new business has found it profitable to set up a Rejection Hotline. Rather than getting your own hands dirty, you can have the company deliver a rejection message like this one, "Accept the fact that you have been rejected, and get over it.

Please do your best to forget about the person who has given us your number because, trust us, he's already forgotten about you." I do not advocate such an approach.

Every moment in dating is either joy or disappointment. If things turn out the way you want, you experience joy. If they don't, you feel disappointment. When you try to avoid the disappointment side, you cut off half the story. Try to see disappointment as a positive experience. As long as you are willing to disappoint others and be disappointed by others, you are free to move through life. When you reject disappointment, you will feel paralyzed and become a prisoner of your own limitations.

How do I deal with sex in my dating relationships?

The answer to this question depends on what personal dating plan you are practicing.

If you are involved in short-term dating, sex plays one role. But if you are considering a long-term commitment, the sexual aspect takes on a much different role.

By answering the following four questions, you will get more clarity about the role of sex in your relationships. After you answer the questions for yourself, I recommend you ask them of your partner.

1. *What am I having sex for?*

I'd be willing to bet that almost no one asks this question, as they're too focused on feelings of sexual attraction and desire. Ask yourself if you want to have sex when your body is heating up, and the answer will be "yes." Asking *what for* will reveal more to you about your dating plan and whether or not you want to go forward with it. It will also slow you down and make you think with something beyond your genitals. When it comes to asking your partner this question, you may feel apprehensive, especially if you haven't known one another for very long. But if you can't even ask your date the question, perhaps you are not ready for the intimacy of having sex!

Sex means different things to different people. For some it is validation, while for others it means caring, love, conquest, security, or strictly release. Once you clarify what you are having sex for, you can decide whether or not you want to participate in sex with your current partner. If any of your dates try to persuade you as to the merits of their purpose, be on the alert.

2. *Can I support the consequences of each sexual encounter?*

This is probably the most vital question of all in the sexual dance, yet one that is also rarely asked, let alone answered. It means being able to accept the consequences that occur when you have sex. These include greater expectations, increased vulnerability, and finding out what the sex relationship is like beyond the fantasy. It lends an added weight to your decision, but it is best for you to decide beforehand if you can handle it, or you'll pay the price. After you and your partner have had sex, the relationship may continue, end, or slowly die out. You need to be open to all three possibilities or prepare to suffer if you are attached to a particular result. While many people may suppose that the issue of consequences only relates to women, the same problem confronts men. Why else would many men slink away after engaging sexually, if they are so comfortable in this area.

The question of supporting sexual involvement breaks down this way: "Can I move ahead sexually regardless of what might happen? Can I allow the disappointment if my expectations aren't met?" If you suspect you can't handle the consequences of a sexual relationship, you are probably not ready for sex. If you are ambivalent, say no.

3. *Do all parts of me want sex?*

Each of us is more than one body. Basically, we are four bodies. The mental body, the emotional body, the physical body, and the spiritual body. Our sexual decision may put these four bodies into

214

conflict with each other because each body has something to say about having sex, and all four may not agree. The emotional body will want to have feelings for the prospective bed partner. The mental body will want to know that this sex partner is someone we can communicate with before, during, and after sex. The physical body will want to experience touching and being touched, and the feeling of being drawn into the other. Last, but not least, the spiritual body will want to feel that there is a connection with this person beyond just a physical release – that there is a higher purpose to the sexual encounter.

Being aware of the status of each of the bodies can be very helpful in avoiding conflict down the road with yourself and your partner.

4 *Is the desire for sex with my partner mutual?*

There are many times you and your partner don't match up in terms of sexual enthusiasm. Try grading your sexual desire for one another on a 1 to 10 scale, which I call the "attraction quotient" How strong is your attraction?

1-2 – Hardly worth it

3-6 - Take it or leave it. Sex will likely be a one-time event

7-8 – Has some strong sexual possibilities.

9-10 – You are in sexual deep water, desire current is really powerful.

Your answers are not written in concrete, but are intended to give you some idea of where you are sexually with a particular person at a given time. As you experience more aspects of your date, it is likely that your response to him or her will change, moving up or down that scale.

Disparity in sexual interest can be especially troublesome when you are the object of someone else's obsessive desire. Many women know exactly how uncomfortable this feels. The bigger issue remains, what can you do about it? You can always refuse with a simple "no" or a somewhat gentler, "I don't feel that way," "I'm not ready," or "I'm not interested."

There is another response, one I call "extending." This asks you to do the opposite of simply opposing your date's assertive desires. Extending is similar to Akido in the martial arts. Instead of trying to resist or block your partner, you step aside to deflect the energy. In Akido, if someone throws a fist, instead of blocking it, you step to the side, take his wrist, and extend his own force until he falls to the ground. This requires much less energy and is especially relevant to dating when there is a lot of thrusting both verbally and physically. For example, one woman asked a sexually assertive date, "When did you first start thinking I was irresistible?" Startled by her directness, he stammered, "I don't know. I guess I thought you were attractive from the beginning."

She followed that with, "Is this something that happens often?" No woman had ever asked him that before, and it turned the tide, especially when she asked, "At what point does the urge seem to subside?" By now the man realized he was way out of his league, and thoughts of being physical with her disappeared. And she hadn't even had to say "no."

How do I know if I am ready to move on?

You will be ready to move on to a new dating plan when you have outgrown your current dating plan, when it no longer serves you in the way it used to. If your need was once for the safety and protection of the *I'm Available to the Unavailable* Dating Plan, but you now have become willing to face your fear and risk trying for more, then it is time for a change.

Another clue that you're ready is when you can leisurely walk away from your current dating plan and approach a new one. This indicates that you are not avoiding your current plan, you are simply ready for a new step. However, if you need to run away from your current dating plan, and you say things like, "I just hate this; this is awful," then you still have some energy for your current dating plan, and some unfinished business there that you need to take care of.

To leave any dating plan, you need to respect it, you need to appreciate what it gave you, and you need to own it and embrace it with full acceptance as I outlined for you in the Steps chapter. Then and only then you'll be able to let it go and move on.

How do I know if my dating plan is successful?

Success of your dating plan is not measured by some external result. Any time you put two feet into a dating plan that reflects who you are, and are accountable for it, you are successful. The dating plan concept is not about proving anything. It is about utilizing what is true for you. There is no comparing in this model, and each plan is respected for what it is and nothing else. There is only one question you need to ask yourself. "Does what I'm doing or saying match the integrity of my chosen plan?"

For example, if you say your dating plan is to find a long-term committed relationship, but you don't trust men, and you're afraid of opening yourself up to scrutiny, accept the fact that you are not ready for the rules of that plan. Trust and openness is a major requirement of an LTCR, as is a willingness to be scared of the vulnerability to which you are opening yourself.

In order to successfully adopt a personal dating plan you need to understand the essence of that plan, follow the rules of that plan, and accept the consequences of that plan. As long as you do so, success is yours, and is not dependent on anything else.

Can I apply the personal dating plan to Internet dating?

Absolutely. The Internet is merely an on-line conduit for people with various personal dating plans to contact one another. The only difference is that you start out anonymously until the first phone call. Each Internet contact will play the same games you would encounter in other kinds of dating. The Internet is a communications device, not a transformer of people.

How do I know if I am in over my head?

If you are not able to follow the rules and accept the consequences that go with your personal dating plan, you are in over your head. This happens often, as many people don't pay attention to the rules, assuming the rules and the consequences don't apply to them. Most are in for a shock.

In general, a long-term relationship will ask you to go slow. However, if speed is your favored choice, you will likely soon find yourself out of control. If someone wants a solid, committed relationship, but insists on over-dramatizing everything that happens along the way, or sets out to create chaos, he or she won't be able to sustain an LTCR for long, and would be better off picking the *High Drama* dating plan and sticking with that.

What if I get bored with my personal dating plan?

No dating plan is inherently boring. You can only get bored if you don't show up for your own plan 100%, or if you're staying in a plan you don't belong. When you're in a plan halfway, hedging and in denial, you will be bored and uncomfortable. Showing up means you put two feet into your plan along with your mental, emotional, physical, and spiritual bodies, and do what it takes to work the dating plan to its fullest. When you do that, you'll find your plan works well and you are not bored.

How can I tell when my partner is telling the truth?

Suppose your date says he is open to an intimate relationship, yet he has never had a relationship that lasted for more than three months. He moves toward you one moment and backs off the next. He says he likes honesty, but he won't share his age or tell you anything about his work. This incongruent behavior is a red flag, and you need to pay attention and trust what you're seeing. When the words and the music don't match, there's a problem. Even if you are not sure of the significance of a particular bit of behavior, if it's incongruent pay attention. Heeding it will serve you well. These signals will slow you down to a walk, and you'll be less apt to stumble.

People who are ambivalent show it through various hedging behaviors, such as being indirect, vague, elusive, or feigning ignorance. These behaviors are fairly easy to recognize and understand. Less obvious are the tactics of someone hiding behind a mask of self-assurance. Early in dating this person may announce, "I don't play games." That is the biggest game of all. Be very suspicious whenever you hear it.

Essentially every partner has two choices—they can be direct and open about their dating plan, or disguise it by wearing a false mask and dodging any direct question. The more each of you play it straight, the less confused you'll be and the more likely you are to enjoy your dating plans. But if protection is the date of choice, then it will be a contest of hedging, slipping, and sliding with truth being a distant memory.

What if my partner is rushing me into an LTCR Dating Plan?

Many couples regard the beginning of a relationship as a track meet. These couples meet and immediately dive into seeing each other every day in the hopes that this is The One. The relationship moves so fast they may get windburn. Within weeks parents are introduced, and if there are children, they are also quickly brought into the mix. The relationship light may burn bright for a while, but soon it begins to dim and the relationship ends as fast as it began.

This often happens to people who haven't dated for a while or haven't dated someone they've been crazy about. Now, by some miracle, a new love is standing in front of them and they feel the need to make up for lost time, so they run past all the stop signs and plunge in. Sex occurs by the second date, discussions of future trips are mentioned in the third, living together in the fourth, and by the fifth they are making plans to see each other every night. The romance and excitement are overwhelming.

They are so caught up they don't bother to ask some very important questions. "Can we sustain this kind of relationship?" "How do you really feel about being committed to a relationship?" "Are you interested in raising children?"

A word of caution for those who frequently find themselves madly in love and convinced that at last, "This is it!" You probably love the feeling of being in love and the idea of meeting that perfect person, but this may not result in your liking the person in front of you. You risk feeling betrayed when the other doesn't cooperate or go along with your lovely fantasy.

What questions can I ask if I want my date to be more revealing?

Any of the following questions will add more depth to your conversations. If your date begs off answering a particular question, his/her refusal will also provide you with clues. All of these questions are very powerful and clearly take you beyond the chit chat of normal dating. Don't even consider asking any of them if you are not ready to raise the tension level or to hear someone get defensive.

Q. What scares you the most about love?

Many people go through their early years feeling unloved in some way, and as a consequence are not prepared to receive love. So they often pick partners who are not able to give love. In that way they don't have to worry about receiving it and can remain within their comfort zone.

Q. What personal traits do you dislike the most in a date?

This question is a great way to get beyond the common facades. Whatever your date dislikes will be a reflection of what unacceptable part your date dislikes within himself.

If he says he hates weakness, be prepared for the great, aggressive cover-up.

Q. What do you find the hardest about dating?

Dating is a mirror that will reveal whatever you don't want to see. If the answer is that your date can't stand to be rejected, this will indicate what your date runs from. If exposing your inadequacies is the answer, then vulnerability will probably be enemy number one.

Q. What is your single greatest flaw?

This is one tough question. Most of us don't want to answer this one, even to ourselves in the privacy of our rooms, let alone to another. Just asking the question will raise the tension level, and you might learn a lot seeing how your date deals with that intensity.

Q. Are you a heartbreaker or the heartbroken?

Ultimately most of us are heartbroken in some fashion. Some prefer to cover this up by breaking other hearts first. That way they don't have to experience anyone leaving them. This is a good question for letting you know how the relationship will play out.

Q. In what way are you the least understood?

Here's where you can expect a lot of defensiveness. If your date feels the least understood about his/her ability to be sexually expressive, he/she will probably be very uncomfortable when this issue is brought up.

Q. Are you able to sustain a love relationship?

Most of us are able to fall in and out of love with great agility. Sustaining love is frequently a much harder task. What woman hasn't heard a man profess great love for her, up to the point of her opening her heart and love? Then like magic his love takes a 180-degree turn, and he is often not heard from again. Sustained love needs to be valued much more than overwhelming intense love.

Q. How do you show your power?

Another way to ask this question would be, "If we were involved, how could I expect you to try to control me?" Don't forget, everyone controls in some way, even you. In cases where your date's response to the question over dinner is "Not at all," and you desire a relationship that involves candidness, openness, and depth get up quietly from the table and leave the restaurant without looking back.

Q. What baffles you the most about women/men?

This question will reveal a gap in an individual's coping style. Typically we struggle with the other sex giving themselves a freedom we don't allow to ourselves. For instance, many women have the freedom to be illogical and irrational. In reaction, men frequently walk around scratching their heads, wondering how in the world could she think that way. On the other side, men have the freedom to withdraw into their caves of silence, activities, or TV. Women, in turn, feel puzzled as to when he will ever get out of his hole and return to the real world.

Q. What do you love about yourself?

In contemplating getting involved with someone, this information is priceless. Perhaps your date loves being intelligent, strong, a great provider, open or witty.

Whatever it is, if you attach yourself to this person, be prepared to experience a steady diet of this quality. It might taste good on date two, but by date 22 you may find yourself craving a different food. Let's say that the person you are considering loves being the helper and can't stand being helpless. If you choose to be with him/her, expect to have someone help you with everything while projecting an image that he/she doesn't need help.

These questions will help you understand who your date truly is, rather than the idealized picture of what you would like him or her to be.

How much should I risk sharing about myself on dates?

Everyone knows, at least to some extent, their bag of unacceptable and undesirable behaviors, traits, and characteristics. "I'm ashamed about being married three times." "Weight has been an issue my entire life." Starting with date one and for many dates after that, the question of how much to expose will do numbers on your head.

Norman started seeing a woman who was twelve years younger than he. Not wanting to add to her concern about the age difference, he did not tell her that he had children. He manipulated all their dates so she never got to see his home with the obvious evidence of children. Ironically, after several months she revealed to him that she had a nine-year-old son. After initially expressing outrage at her deception, he confessed to her that he also had children; in fact he had two!

Overall, we are extremely hesitant to let out any of our unacceptable characteristics or details, not trusting that our dates can handle them, and wondering if it will drive them off. If safety were our only concern, we would most likely decide never to share any of these so-called flaws. However, in protecting our images by monitoring what we show, there is a concern that we will appear closed off to our dates. We often try to rationalize this any way we can in order to delay the exposure and the possible humiliation or rejection. We think, "Best to wait until a later date," "He/she wouldn't understand," or "Maybe it won't come up."

Whether you share or not is also dependent on the consequences you are willing to live with. If you can't stand being guarded and careful all the time, it's best for you to Share. If you believe sharing will blow the relationship, you might prefer not to share. If you only want a partner who can accept all of you, then sharing will be highly valued. If you are too embarrassed to expose who you are, you probably won't share.

How much interest can I reveal to my dates?

You may feel you need to be extremely careful not to show too much interest for fear your dates will reject you or get the wrong idea and accuse you later of leading them on. A third concern is if the other person realizes we like him/her, we may be considered too needy. Most people lean toward the side of caution and hold their interest back.

What you do will depend on how much you like being true to yourself. If you are the kind of person who always seeks the votes of others, you will be very cautious about revealing your interest, and will likely wait until you sense that the vote will be in your favor. If you don't live for others' approval, you may throw caution to the wind and state, "I am interested in you, period."

How much freedom can I allow myself in being me?

You've read the books, you've talked to your friends, and you've seen the movies, so you know by now the expected roles you are supposed to play. The problem is that often who you are doesn't fit those roles, and you may have trouble playing them. Let's say you are basically a sweet, nice guy, but you feel most women, despite their lip service about liking sensitive men, really want the confident, self-assured, ambitious types. Or suppose you are a naturally bright, aggressive, outspoken woman who's been warned to play dumb and be quiet lest you intimidate and alienate your man. What do you do? Do you try to protect yourself or do you let your date see who you really are?

Again, it depends on whether you want to live your truth and embrace words like allow, permission, accept, and integrity, or prefer to be run by what others say.

PART VI

THE GRADES

CHAPTER 20

 THE DATING REPORT CARD

Here is where you need to face, once and for all, the reality that dating is about judgments – both receiving and giving them. There is no way around this judgmental gauntlet unless you prefer pretending. As long as you choose to enter the dating arena and select a dating plan, no matter which one you participate in, it will ask you to reject anyone who doesn't fit the plan or be rejected by anyone who doesn't want to play your plan with you.

The whole purpose of the Personal Dating Plan concept is to make dating a conscious experience instead of an unconscious effort to keep judgments hidden and avoid any awareness of what's really going on.

Connor was very attracted to Serena at their first meeting. There was no indication that the feeling was mutual, but Serena seemed to display an initial enthusiasm for their getting together at the start of the date. About halfway through the date there was an edge to her responses when Connor shared his perspectives on life. From that point on the conversation seemed stilted. Since Connor still found Serena bright and physically attractive, he asked her out again. They agreed to go to the movies, but during dinner the initial concerns became even more apparent and the conversation dragged. Neither of them chose to address the difficulty, and Connor remained puzzled about the nature of the impasse. Though his eyes led him to want more, it was hopeless. There was barely enough interest to finish the second date, and definitely not enough to support a third. As with most dates, it was the unspoken issues that dragged them down. It could have ended more enjoyably if Connor had risked bringing up the obvious and said, "It seems clear that you've made some negative judgments about me that has led to your disinterest and the end of our brief dating. You can keep them to yourself or you can make this date more interesting by telling me what they are, since we won't be seeing each other again anyway. I certainly won't hold it against you."

In this chapter you'll fill out *The Dating Report Card*, a process that will help both you and your partner learn how to date without your facades, and give each other honest feedback that will level the dating playing field. Afterward, instead of continuing to date in the dark, you'll be dealing moment to moment with what's really going on between you and the person you're with.

After you spend some time with a potential partner, the two of you can evaluate what's going on by writing down your judgments about the other – positive or negative, fair or not fair, accurate or not – in answer to the fifty questions on *The Dating Report Card.* In response to each question, give two grades (A,B,C,D, or F), one grade for yourself and one for your date. The answers will give you both a clearer picture of what this potential match is all about.

Let's say that on your report card you decide to give yourself an "A" for your energy level, but you give your date only a "C." What does this tell you about your future together? It says you will probably have to be the one who keeps pumping juice into the relationship and possibly end up feeling frustrated when you realize the burden of carrying the relationship rests on you. Or let's say you spot some major inconsistencies.

You know you value emotional availability, authenticity, and depth, but in filling out the *Dating Report Card,* you see there is no evidence of these traits in your date. Now you know you have a mismatch.

To Share or Not to Share

After filling out *The Dating Report Card,* you may choose to share your judgments with one another or not. If you decide to share your answers, do so with grace and respect. Otherwise keep them to yourself.

Difficult as it may be to share judgments, the benefits will delight you. Imagine the freedom of no longer needing to defend your powerlessness, insecurities, fears, and inadequacies. Imagine walking away from a date, whether you decide to see each other again or not, and actually know what happened between you!

Honesty by Mutual Agreement

The Dating Report Card is not about indulging in honesty for its own sake or using it to hurt others. It is honesty by mutual agreement. There will be no judgment sharing unless both parties agree to it. If there is no such agreement, I recommend you keep your answers to yourself.

The purpose of *The Dating Report Card* is to further raise your consciousness and provide you with a tool to help you determine who is the best possible partner for your current dating plan. The whole dating game changes whenever you make consciousness, rather than results, your goal. *The Dating Report Card* creates a place for sincerity and respect. It enables you to communicate clearly with your partner about your needs, interests, and desires. It's a way to get beyond the nebulous sharing that usually takes place. With *The Dating Report Card,* you have enough evidence to enable you to decide if this partner is a good match or simply doesn't fit into your dating plan.

Why Some People Don't Like Using *The Dating Report Card*

When it comes to giving honest feedback to others, the voices in our head censor us. They tell us we will hurt the other person's feelings or that it will hurt our image of ourselves as a nice person.

Also, there is a lot of discomfort stirred up when we share judgments that will likely be viewed as negative. How can a woman tell a man that he's too short, or that he seems to be so in love with himself, it would be a crime to break the two of him up? How can a man tell a woman she's not sexy enough or she's too old?

Maybe you think, "I'm only secretive with someone I don't like." Strangely enough, that's not usually how it works. When we like someone, we're tempted to hide out even more for fear that if we are upfront, we'll send them running. In either case, instead of being direct, our minds lock into how to get through the date without exposing our judgments of the other or having to hear our date's judgments of us.

What you decide to do depends on how you want to be treated. Do you want to be treated as a clueless, rejected, discarded object? Or would you rather be enlightened by honest feedback so you can learn from it and increase your chances of a better match next time out?

You don't need to be loud and aggressive, just speak your truth in a quiet, gentle way.

If the other person gets defensive, your honesty probably struck a chord and may not be appreciated. No need for debate. Just move on and keep looking until you find someone who is on the same wavelength you are.

Male/Female Reactions

One of the assumptions about *The Dating Report Card* is that it's harder for women to use than men. This may be based on the assumption that women are more sensitive than men. But men can be just as hurt by judgments as women, though they may not articulate it for fear of sounding weak. Another assumption is that it's harder for women, with their nurturing natures, to say anything that might hurt a man. This may be the case when the woman is dealing with a passive hiding little boy or a puffed up little boy, who gets pouty or explosive when criticized. But real men can take it. I want to encourage the women who read this book to practice relating to a man's higher nature. Instead of trying to play it safe with a man, gracefully invite him to meet you on the level playing field of openness and honesty. This will eventually raise your own level of consciousness about relationships, and will result in you attracting partners who have a deeper respect for who you are, instead of seeing you as an object to be controlled or a mother figure.

The Choice is Yours

Keep in mind that on a date you always have two options. You can either use the material that you have gathered for your own enlightenment, or you can open up a dialogue about it with your date. That may mean you risk rejection on the spot, or enjoy the possibility of transforming the relationship into something much, much better.

Which path should you take? That's up to you – how comfortable you are exchanging information openly and playing with the judgments both of you make from the moment you first see each other. When you share your inner dialogue with your dates, using the structure of *The Dating Report Card*, your dating experiences can become more meaningful and satisfying, and you will develop a warm compassion for each other's struggles.

How to Fill In *The Dating Report Card*

Invite your date to fill out one copy of *The Dating Report Card* while you fill out he other. You can even do this in a restaurant over coffee. The answers will provide a summary of how you view one another. You can decide to show each other your answers or not. Just realize that the value of *The Dating Report Card* is nullified if not filled out honestly.

Grades

In response to each question, grade yourself and your date as follows:

A = if the quality is just how you like it

B = if the quality is close, but not quite up to par

C = if the quality is merely OK, but doesn't really excite you

D = if the quality is clearly below your standards

E = if the quality doesn't exist for you at all

There is also a space below each question for comments, in case you want to put down additional details.

I repeat that the sharing of *Dating Report Cards* is a joint venture. Both of you need to agree beforehand, "I'll show you mine if you show me yours." If you go ahead without this agreement, the report card will be seen as abusive and intrusive. Respect your date's desire to share or not to share. Let it be a free choice. Also agree on when this sharing will take place. After the first date? Third date? Never? If it's never, you can still fill it out and hold on to the answers. You can benefit by thinking about the material discussed in this book and applying it as it suits your needs.

Now let's look at *The Dating Report Card*

The Dating Report Card

Question	Your Grade	Date's Grade

Age: _____

    Comment _____

Height: _____

    Comment _____

Weight _____

    Comment _____

Looks _____

    Comment _____

Build_____

    Comment _____

Intelligence _____

    Comment _____

Social Maturity _____

    Comment _____

Sense of Humor _____

    Comment _____

Ability to Articulate_____

    Comment _____

Ability to Engage in Dialogue _____

    Comment _____

Awareness of World Events _____

WE COULD'VE HAD A GREAT DATE
IF IT WEREN'T FOR YOU

    Comment _____

Self Awareness _____

    Comment _____

Interests _____

    Comment _____

Career_____

    Comment _____

Level of Success _____

    Comment _____

Athletic Skills _____

    Comment _____

Personality _____

    Comment _____

Excitement Level_____

    Comment _____

Integrity and Trust Level _____

    Comment _____

Stability _____

    Comment _____

Capacity for Compassion and Love_____

    Comment _____

Sense of Autonomy and Freedom _____

    Comment _____

Masculine/Feminine Qualities_____

    Comment _____

Independence _____

    Comment _____

Generosity _____

    Comment _____

Level of Relationship Commitment _____

    Comment _____

Primary Values _____

    Comment _____

Red Flags _____

    Comment _____

Sense of Family _____

    Comment _____

Network Including Relatives/Friends _____

    Comment _____

Ambition _____

    Comment _____

Intensity _____

    Comment _____

Financial Success _____

    Comment _____

Creativity _____

    Comment _____

Manner of movement and rhythm _____

    Comment _____

Style of dress _____

Comment _____

Compatibility _____

    Comment _____

Physical Health _____

    Comment _____

Emotional Health_____

    Comment _____

Emotional Availability_____

    Comment _____

Package, Including Kids and Ex-Spouses _____

    Comment _____

Ability to Listen_____

    Comment _____

Ability to Discuss the Relationship _____

    Comment _____

Ability to Communicate Feelings _____

    Comment _____

Reliability _____

    Comment _____

Soul Connection_____

    Comment _____

Sexual Connection_____

    Comment _____

Depth and Substance _____

    Comment _____

Honesty and Authenticity _____

    Comment _____

Ability to Handle Conflict _____

    Comment _____

Sense of Responsibility _____

    Comment _____

Overall Chemistry _____

    Comment _____

Level of Interest in Friendship Dating_____

    Comment _____

Level of Interest in Serious Love Relationship _____

Other Comments _____

_____

_____

_____

And Now...

As you venture forth into the world of conscious, accountable dating, keep these things in mind:

- Recognize and be accountable for your current dating plan
- Embrace your plan 100%
- Only select someone who fits your plan
- Honor the integrity of your plan through thought and action
- Be aware of any red flags
- Be alert to if or when you are ready to move beyond your current plan

And enjoy the process!!

BIBLIOGRAPHY

Atwood, Nina: Be Your Own Dating Service
New York, Henry Holt, 1996

Carter, Steven: Men Who Can't Love
New York, Berkley Books, 1989

Farrell, Warren: Why Men Are The Way They Are
New York, Berkley Books,1988

Ford, Debbie: The Dark Side Of The Light Chasers
New York, Penquin, 1998

Friedman, Edwin: Friedman's Fables
New York, Guilford, 1985

Krasnow, Iris: Surrendering To Marriage
New York, Hyperion, 2001

McCann, Eileen: The Two Step: The Dance Of Intimacy
Grove Press, 1987

O'Hanlon, John: I Guide To Inclusive Therapy
New York, /W.W. Norton, 2003

Rhodes, S. Cold Feet: Why Men Don't Commit
New York, Penguin, 1989

Shmuley, Boteach: Why Can't I Fall In Love
New York, Harper Collins, 2001

Sterling, Justin: What Really Works With Men
New York, Warner Books, 1992

Tessina, Tina: The Unofficial Guide To Dating Again
New York, Macmillan, 1998

Contact information

For those who resonate to the philosophy and therapeutic methods presented here and desire further involvement through workshops, lectures, groups or private sessions please contact me by sending me the following information.

Bruce Derman, Ph.D.
S-806
22817 Ventura Blvd.
Woodland Hills, Ca. 91364

(818) 375-7194

Name:_____

Address:_____

City:_____State:_____Zip:_____

Telephone: (   ) _____

Interest:_____

ABOUT THE AUTHOR

Bruce Derman, Ph.D. is a licensed clinical psychologist in private practice for over 35 years in Woodland Hills and Santa Monica, Ca., who specializes in working with people in all stages of relationship, especially couples in conflict and singles desiring a change in their dating pattern. He is also a divorce mediator, trainer and coach for the Coalition for Collaborative Divorce and child custody mediator and evaluator with the San Fernando Valley Child Custody Center. His previous book was entitled WE'D HAVE A GREAT RELATIONSHIP IF IT WEREN'T FOR YOU.

Printed in the United States
52795LVS00006B/1-102

9 781410 793355